I0816646

ICELANDIC
MITTENS

Guðrún Hannele Henttinen

ICELANDIC MITTENS

25 Traditional Patterns Reimagined

Trafalgar Square
North Pomfret, Vermont

First published in the United States of America
in 2021 by
Trafalgar Square Books
North Pomfret, Vermont 05053

Originally published in Icelandic as *Íslenskir vettlingar*.

ISBN 978-1-64601-107-0
Library of Congress Control Number: 2021941830

Editor: Oddný S. Jónsdóttir/Forlagið
Design and Layout: Alexandra Buhl/Forlagið
Photos: Gígja Einarsdóttir,
page 6 Guðrún Hannele Henttinen,
page 10 Einar Einarsson (1903–1962)
© Reykjavik Museum of Photography,
page 13 Ásgrímur Ágústsson © Akureyri Museum
Illustrations: Anna Cynthia Leplar

Printed in China
10 9 8 7 6 5 4 3 2 1

TABLE OF CONTENTS

INTRODUCTION

My love of mittens is longstanding, and I'm always quick to take notice when someone is wearing a beautiful pair. The primary purpose of mittens is, of course, to keep your hands warm, but the way they look matters, too. A pair of well-knitted, beautifully patterned mittens made from good yarn is a treasure to be used and enjoyed for years. All sorts of needlework treasures are hidden away in the Textile Museum in Blönduós, which is where I found the mittens in this book—all 25 beautiful and interesting pairs. I'm forever grateful to Museum Director Elín S. Sigurðardóttir for her co-operation. The book contains photographs of the original mittens, which are followed by patterns that have been adapted to suit fingering weight yarn for needles US size 0 to 1.5 (2 to 2.5 mm). The mittens are also shown in different colours for inspiration.

I have tried to ensure a diverse range of mittens in my selection, both in terms of knitting techniques and patterns, to include mittens that are suitable for beginners as well as seasoned knitters. In many people's estimation, stranded knitting produces characteristically Icelandic mittens. But the technique can be used in all sorts of different ways—for patterns on the backs or palms of mittens, the same pattern for the whole body of the mitten, mittens with ribbed or two-colored or lace pattern cuffs, afterthought thumbs, thumbs attached on the palm or on the side, and mittens with or without thumb gussets. I also added two pairs of solid-color mittens with lace patterns and two pairs of gloves. Everyone should be able to find a knitting project of interest to them.

Putting together a book like this is a marathon project, and many people have lent a helping hand. The brainstorming for the book started in good cooperation with Cindy. Her contribution and encouragement has been invaluable. The book would not have been made without the help of Elín at the Textile Museum in Blönduós. I also had the assistance of several talented knitters: Guðný, Margrét, Rannveig, and Sonja. Cindy also knitted a pair of mittens. My sincerest thanks to all of you!

Much credit goes to Gígja, the photographer, who took all the photographs. Thank you for your artistic eye, Gígja!

I thank models Elín Eva and Lamie for their hard work. My daughter Elín Eva deserves special thanks for taking on the role of stylist and doing it so well, and for being patient with her mother during all the photo shoots.

And, of course, I thank editor Oddný S. Jónsdóttir, graphic designer Alexandra Buhl, and technical editor Kirsten Pedrosa for their essential work on this project.

Last but not least, I must thank my husband Karl for supporting me in this endeavor, as well as my whole family.

Happy knitting!
Guðrún Hannele Henttinen

A BRIEF HISTORY OF KNITTING IN ICELAND

It's thought that knitting came to Iceland with merchants from the Netherlands, England, or Germany in the first part of the 16th century, and that Icelanders may even have learned to knit earlier than other Nordic peoples. The oldest knitted garment that still exists today in Iceland is a mitten. It was found during an archeological excavation at the Stóra-Borg Farm in South Iceland, and is thought to date back to the early 16th century. The mitten was knitted in stocking stitch in the round with four or five double-pointed needles in a small adult size. Finding it was a stroke of luck because garments made of wool and other textiles are short-lived—they are made to be used, they fray and wear out, and then the yarn is reused as long as possible. Because people saw no reason to preserve everyday knitted garments, we have very few clues to help us trace the history of knitting in Iceland.

We know that Icelanders throughout the country were quick to take up knitting, which was much simpler to master than the weaving widely practiced at the time. Compared to weaving, knitting is easier to learn, the necessary tools are much simpler, and it takes up less space. It is also faster than *nålebinding* or "knotless knitting," a technique that Icelanders had previously used to make mittens.

In the beginning, Icelanders only used knit stitches, as the mitten from Stóra-Borg indicates. Later, in the 18th century, people started to make use of purl stitches as well. Garments were mostly made from yarn in all the natural colors of the Icelandic sheep.

Knitted mittens, socks, and other garments became important export products in the 19th century. In order to increase production, people were assigned piecework tasks, and each person in a household was obliged to knit a certain amount every week. An industrious farmwoman, for instance, would be expected to knit one pair of socks a day, or card and spin enough yarn for one sock and then knit it. Children as young as eight had to knit two pairs of fishermen's mittens every week. Men often had to work with the coarsest wool, while women processed the fine wool and did more delicate needlework, such as knitting intricate patterns or lacework. There are even anecdotes about guests being asked to knit, as idleness was frowned upon.

Where did the mitten designs and patterns come from? Experienced knitters probably each had their own basic mitten pattern. New designs would have been passed between people and farms in various ways. When a guest arrived wearing a knitted garment with an interesting design, for instance, a copy would be made of the pattern. Once written down, patterns were passed from generation to generation and also obtained from abroad. In more recent times, printed books and magazines with patterns became available. The founding of schools for women teaching domestic subjects in the latter part of the 19th century undoubtedly had an influence on what Icelanders knitted.

There is little information to be had about many of the mittens in this book: whether they are the knitters' original designs or whether the ideas for them came from somewhere else. Patterns and designs often traveled widely, making it difficult to trace their origins; the concept of "design" simply didn't exist at the time. We do know, however, that certain knitters specialized in knitting mittens with specific designs that they produced in their own unique style.

HEIMILISIÐNAÐARSAFNIÐ
TEXTILE MUSEUM

THE TEXTILE MUSEUM IN BLÖNDUÓS

The story of the Textile Museum in Blönduós dates back to the 1970s, when it was established thanks to the collaboration of local Women's Association chapters in the region. In 1976, the museum formally opened to the public—at the time, housed in an old barn and cowshed belonging to the Blönduós Women's Domestic College. However, the museum soon outgrew its humble accommodations, and in 2003 a new and larger museum connected to the original building was opened. All of the original mittens on which the patterns in this book are based are preserved in the Textile Museum's permanent collection.

ICELANDIC WOOL

The museum's Wool Exhibition demonstrates the process that wool goes through from fleece to finished garment. Museum visitors can feel different types of wool for themselves and see how they vary. For instance, *þel*, an underwool unique to Icelandic sheep, consists of short fibers that are incredibly soft and fine, and forms the warm, dry layer closest to the sheep's skin. *Tog* is the longer and coarser wool that Icelandic sheep grow as an outer layer. Traditionally, Icelandic wool was hand-processed, and the *tog* separated from the *þel*. This done, two kinds of yarn were spun. The museum's woolens exhibition includes examples of beautiful shawls knitted from both *tog* and *þel*. The yarn is handspun and delicate, and each type—*tog* and *þel*—has its own characteristics and beauty. The museum collection includes numerous other items made from wool, such as mittens made using twined and lacework knitting techniques and rougher work mittens.

HALLDÓRUSTOFA

Halldórustofa is a special wing of the museum named for Halldóra Bjarnadóttir (1873–1981), a trailblazer in the field of handcrafts who worked tirelessly to promote women's education and culture in the 20th century.

Halldóra completed a teacher's certificate in Norway in 1899 and taught in Reykjavík and Norway before later becoming the headmistress of Akureyri Primary School in North Iceland. She saw to it that handcrafts were not only taught but were part of the basic curriculum for primary and secondary school students throughout the country. She became a handcrafts consultant and received special grant funding for her efforts in this work from 1924 to 1955. In 1946, Halldóra founded a Wool and Textile College at Svalbarð in Eyjafjörður,

North Iceland, which she oversaw for nine years. She was also the editor of the journal *Hlín* for almost 50 years.

Halldóra worked to preserve age-old knowledge of materials and methods, develop new techniques, and increase the value of Icelandic wool. During the first half of the 20th century, she staged several exhibitions throughout the country which displayed Icelandic handcrafts and placed special emphasis on the myriad possibilities for using Icelandic wool. Textiles, knitted mittens, socks, and shawls were often among the items on display. Halldóra collected samples and examples of all kinds of textile objects that are still held in the museum's collection.

Halldóra lived out the last years of her life in Blönduós and bequeathed to the Textile Museum her final possessions, which are on display in Halldórustofa.

MUSEUM EXHIBITIONS

The museum has many permanent exhibitions, among them exhibitions of embroidery, Iceland's national costumes, and wool. Every summer there are also special exhibitions in which contemporary designers and textile artists are given the opportunity to display the diversity of Icelandic handcraft and design.

A visit to the Textile Museum offers a broad variety of insights into Iceland's textile history, particularly Icelandic women's handcrafts. Wool is interwoven with Icelandic history and culture, and there are many treasures to be found in the museum's collection, among them the hand-knitted mittens made from delicate, handspun yarn which inspired the mitten patterns in this book.

knitters rule!
cm
inch
HANDPRJONAD

TECHNICAL INFORMATION

ABBREVIATIONS

CC = contrast color

cm = centimeter(s)

CO = cast on

DPN(s) = double-pointed needle(s)

g = grams

in = inch(es)

inc = increase

incl = including

k = knit

k1tbl = knit 1 stitch through the back loop

k2tog = knit two stitches together by knitting them both at the same time. One stitch decreased.

kfb = increase by knitting twice into the same stitch. First, through the front as in a knit stitch and then, without slipping it off the left needle, knit into the back of the stitch and then slip it off the needle. One stitch increased.

kfbf = increase by knitting three times into the same stitch. First, through the front as in a knit stitch and then, without slipping it off the left needle, knit into the back of the stitch and finally, knit through the front again and then slip it off the needle. Two stitches increased.

M1L = pick up the bar between the last stitch you knitted and the one you are about to knit, inserting the needle from front to back. Then knit into the back of this stitch. One stitch increased.

M1R = pick up the bar between the last stitch you knitted and the one you are about to knit, inserting the needle from back to front. Then knit into the front of this stitch. One stitch increased.

mm = millimeter(s)

p = purl

pm = place marker

rnd = round

RS = right side

sl1, k2tog, psso = slip one stitch knitwise, knit the next 2 stitches together, then pass the slipped stitch over the 2 knit together stitches. Two stitches decreased.

sl2tog, k1, p2sso = slip 2 stitches knitwise *at the same time*, knit one, then pass the slipped stitches over. The middle stitch will be on top. Two stitches decreased.

sm = slip marker

ssk = slip 2 stitches knitwise one at a time, insert the left needle through both stitches in front of the right needle and knit them together through the back loop.

st(s) = stitch(es)

WS = wrong side

yo = yarnover increase. To work a yarnover increase, bring the yarn over the right hand needle from front to back, and then into position to work the next stitch. This creates a hole and a new stitch, and is used in lace knitting. A decrease, i.e. two stitches knit together, is often paired with this increase to keep the amount of stitches the same over the round. On the next round, the YO is worked as any other stitch.

REPEAT

[...] = work instructions within brackets as many times as directed

- = repeat instructions between asterisks as many times as directed

**** or *** or ****** = indicate a place in a pattern to begin a section

ICELANDIC KNITTING TECHNIQUES

In Iceland, we use the continental knitting method. We have a long tradition of knitting mittens in the round, mainly using 5 double-pointed needles. We hold both needles the same way in both hands and use them almost equally. The yarn lies from the stitch just knitted on the right needle over the index finger on the left hand. In stranded knitting, the second strand of yarn lies over the middle finger. We like to think that this results in fast knitting, which is good when you knit a lot. If you are used to a different knitting method, however, do not let the descriptions of the continental knitting method confuse you. All knitting methods give the same result. Just knit as you are used to and the outcome will be practically the same or very similar.

YARN

The original mittens which provided the inspiration for this book were knitted with a fine home-spun wool that is difficult to replicate exactly today. All the modern yarns chosen for the new mittens are 100% wool, with one exception where silk is used.

Pirrkalanka is a traditional 4-ply woollen yarn of fingering weight. It is ideally suited for the tight knitting of traditional Icelandic mittens and fills the stitches up nicely. It is strong and pills very little.

Fine Tweed is not as stretchy but fills the stitches up beautifully. This type of yarn felts easily, which can give traditional patterns a lovely look. It makes lightweight and warm mittens.

Mohair 2-ply is a mixture of mohair and merino wool. Although classified as sport-weight, it is a soft spun yarn also suitable for tight knitting on finer needles. The mohair gives a beautiful sheen to a pair of your best mittens, and at the same time is very warm. Mittens worked in this yarn will be soft but keep their shape well.

See a list of yarns for mittens on pages 269–270.

CHOOSING A SUBSTITUTE YARN

Choosing the right sort of wool for knitting mittens is important. Remember that mittens must be more durable than most other knitted items. Mittens are used in all types of weather—in snow and rain—and endure lots of rubbing and friction.

Wool is warm, which is the main *raison d'être* for mittens—to keep your hands warm. If the wool used is not superwash wool, then the mittens will have a tendency to felt with time and use, and will in fact become warmer. Superwash wool doesn't felt as much and won't become as dense.

All kinds of wool yarn can be used for mittens, but mittens made from worsted spun yarn with a tight twist are stronger, will last longer, and are less likely to pill; on the other hand, they are not as warm. Mittens from woolen spun yarn are likely to be more dense and felt more with use. That helps to make them durable, and although the yarn itself is not as strong, they are lighter and warmer. So the choice is up to the knitter. One suggestion is to try both and decide for yourself.

Try to choose wool that fills the stitches well and makes stranded projects knitting more even. It's much more enjoyable to knit stranded with yarn like that. Also keep in mind that really soft yarn can also be limp, and therefore not as suitable for mittens.

PARTS OF THE MITTEN

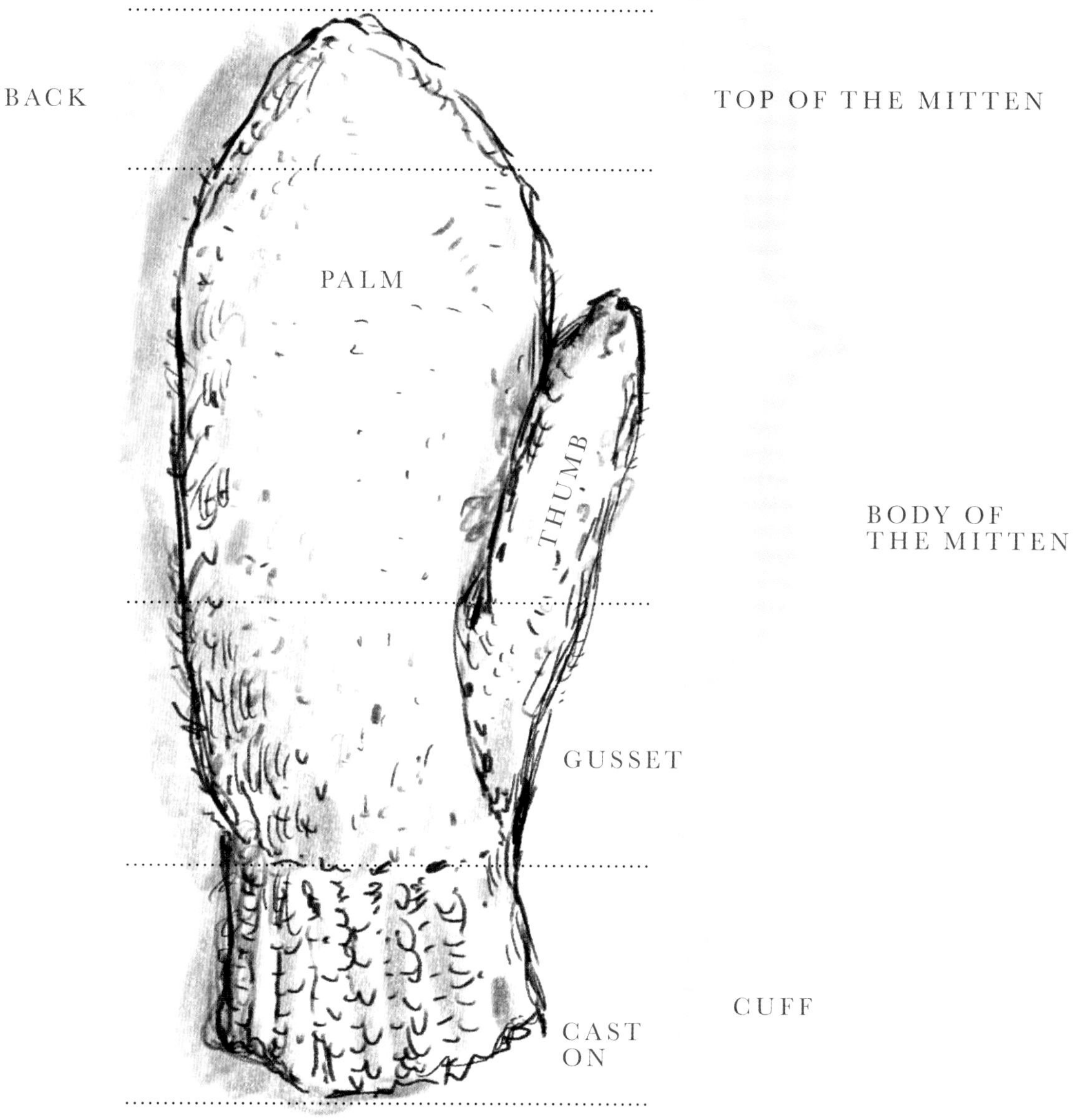

BACK

TOP OF THE MITTEN

PALM

THUMB

BODY OF THE MITTEN

GUSSET

CUFF

CAST ON

CUFF

CAST ON

Where stitches are cast on and knitting starts.

CUFF

Different names are used for different parts of the mittens in the instructions. At the bottom or covering the wrist is the cuff. The cuff is either worked in a rib stitch or with a two-color or lace pattern.

THUMB

AFTERTHOUGHT THUMB

Afterthought thumb

While working the body of the mitten, an opening for the thumb is made by first knitting the thumb stitches (the width of the thumb) with a piece of scrap yarn of a contrasting color. Then these stitches are worked with the main color on the next round of knitting. When the body of the mitten is complete, the scrap yarn is pulled out and the live stitches placed on at least three DPNs. An alternate method is to thread the DPNs through the stitches before the scrap yarn is pulled out. Be aware that the there will be one stitch less on the top of the thumb opening created in this way than on the bottom, since it is actually the spaces between stitches that are being picked up from the top of the opening. This is resolved by picking up one extra stitch next to the top stitches, which makes the number of stitches equal on the top and bottom of the thumb.

Thumb with a gusset

Mittens usually have the thumb gusset on the palm side of the mitten or on the side of the hand. The gusset is triangular and is usually worked straight after the cuff, at the beginning of the body of the mitten. The thumb is worked from the live stitches at the top of the gusset. A gusset adds more width to the part of the mitten below the thumb.

PALM THUMB WITH GUSSET

Palm thumb with gusset

When the mitten is patterned, a special pattern chart is included for the thumb gusset. It has to be followed *at the same time* as the pattern for the body of the mitten. When the gusset is completed, the stitches are placed on a short length of scrap yarn and new stitches are cast on above the thumb opening, usually fewer in number than the gusset stitches. When the body of the mitten is complete, the thumb is created from the gusset stitches, the stitches picked up behind the gusset, and new stitches picked up on either side of the gusset.

SIDE THUMB WITH GUSSET

Side thumb with gusset

The gusset for a side thumb is worked on the side of the mitten. It is often wider than a gusset knit on the palm. Increases are started at the end of the cuff or beginning of the body. The advantage of this type of thumb is that left and right mittens are interchangeable (unless of course there are different patterns on the front and back of the mitten).

GUSSET BEHIND THE THUMB

Gusset behind the thumb

Extra stitches behind the thumb can also form an inner gusset. These stitches are decreased gradually to create a triangle. In patterned mittens, this gusset has its own chart to follow.

BODY OF THE MITTEN — From the cuff to the top of the mitten and all the way around.

PALM — The inside part of the mitten on the palm, from the cuff to the top of the mitten. This part of the mitten gets the most wear and is often worked in its own pattern.

BACK — The outside part of the mitten on the back of the hand, from the cuff to the top. This part is more visible and often worked in its own pattern.

TOP OF THE MITTEN — Starts where the decreases begin.

READING CHARTS

Charts usually only show the right side of a mitten or pattern. All mittens in this book except one pair are knitted in the round. Therefore, each round is read from right to left, i.e. in the same direction as you knit.

SIZES

As mentioned earlier, the original mittens were knitted using very fine yarn, often hand-spun. The new versions of these mittens are knitted in a slightly larger gauge using fingering/4-ply wool and size US 0/2 mm or US 1/2.5 mm needles.

All the mitten patterns in this book are one size—women's medium. It is easy to change the sizing without affecting the patterns in the charts. Each mitten has a gauge given, but if slightly larger needles and/or heavier wool is used for a looser gauge, the mittens will be larger; if smaller needles and/or finer wool is used for a tighter gauge, they will be smaller. Please keep in mind that changing the gauge can have an effect on the density and the appearance of the mittens.

If the intended wearer can try on the mitten as it is being knitted, it is good to check whether the decreases in the patterns for the thumb and/or individual fingers begin when the knitting reaches the middle of the nails. The decreases for the top of the mitten begin when the mitten has reached the top of the little finger.

GAUGE

Getting the right gauge is essential when knitting mittens or gloves of a specific size. To ensure the right size, it's important to knit a gauge swatch. Remember that two-color knitting can be tighter than plain stocking stitch. Various things can affect the gauge. Smooth and silky yarn can be more difficult to knit. Certain types of needles can make knitting looser. Most knitters knit more tightly on less-smooth needles, such as bamboo needles or square needles.

Generally speaking, it's best to knit mittens or gloves tightly because that way they will be warmer and last longer.

MAKING A GAUGE SWATCH

Basic swatch

Usually a square swatch of 5.5–6 in/14–16 cm is worked to test the pattern gauge of stitches per 4 in/10 cm. The gauge won't be as accurate if the swatch is smaller and the measurement extends right to its edges. Knitting the first 2 or 3 stitches in garter stitch prevents the edges from rolling. The middle stitches are worked in the stitch used in the mitten pattern. To obtain the most accurate gauge, wash and block the swatch before measuring.

Swatch knit in two colors in the round—stranded colorwork
Because these mittens are worked in the round, it can be more accurate to also work the swatch in the round. Many knitters knit more tightly and evenly in the round than when working flat. It's possible to work a square swatch of stranded knitting in the round from right to left without closing each round. This can be done by letting the yarn lie loosely across the back so the next round can be started again from the right. This method ensures a more even gauge, but a tubular gauge swatch can also be worked in rounds with DPNs. Make sure there are enough stitches to allow you to measure at least 2.5 in/5 cm of flat fabric if working a tubular swatch. To obtain the most accurate gauge, wash and block the swatch before measuring.

Picking up stitches on side of thumb

Two stitches are picked up and knitted on each side of thumb. Take care to avoid a gap where those stitches are picked up. If it is hard to fill a possible gap with two stitches, you can pick up one extra stitch on each side and then decrease them away immediately on the next round.

NEEDLES

Double-pointed needles (in a set of five) are called for in the instructions. These are most commonly used for knitting socks, mittens, and gloves, and other objects worked in the round with a small diameter. The mitten stitches are held on four needles (or three if you prefer) and the fifth (or fourth) is used as the working needle. The thumb stitches are distributed on three needles and worked with the fourth. Double-pointed needles 6 in/15 cm long are very comfortable, and are available in a large selection of different materials such as aluminium, birch, bamboo, and more.

Two circular needles can also be used to knit in the round. The length of the circular needles may vary, but this technique is easier if they are shorter. If two circular needles are used, the number of stitches is distributed across both needles—the back of the hand on one needle and the palm on the other. The same stitches are always worked with the same needles so that they never move across needles.

One long circular needle is used for the magic loop method of knitting in the round. The needle has to be at least 32 in/80 cm long; you can find this method explained and demonstrated on various websites.

Flexible double-pointed needles are specifically designed for sock and mitten knitting and even for sleeves worked in the round. The stitches are distributed across two needles—the back of the hand on one needle and the palm on the other. Then you knit with the third. Many knitters find these needles very useful in eliminating the loose stitches and laddering that can occur between double-pointed needles.

CAST ONS

Twisted German cast-on

This method is highly recommended when casting on mittens. It produces a thick, strong, elastic edge.

Knitted cast-on

A simple cast-on which is useful when the cast-on edge needs to be finer and only one strand of yarn is available. Good for casting on stitches behind the thumb opening.

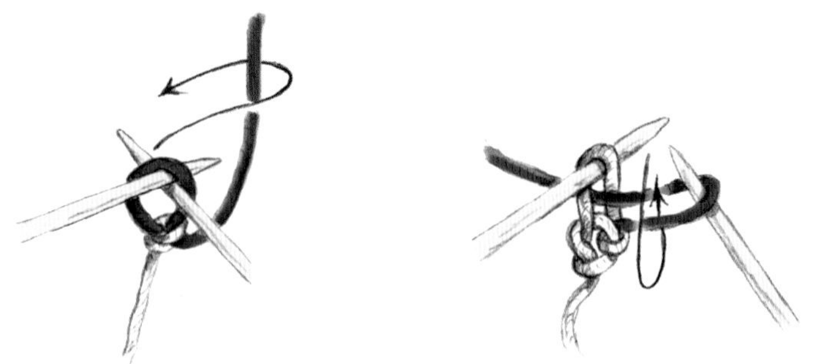

These methods are demonstrated in videos on the website: reykjavikknittingcompany.com

RIBBING

Most of the cuffs in this book are worked in ribbing, either k1, p1 or k2, p2, or variations of these. The more stitches there are in each rib, the less elastic the cuff.

Twisted knit stitch

Work the knit stitches in the ribbing through the back loop (twisted) if the cuff needs to be firmer. The twisted stitches will be slightly raised on the RS of the cuff.

You also have the option of working the purl stitch twisted. This is useful if you want the cuff to be tighter without the twisted stitch being visible from the right side of the mitten.

Arranging the stitches on the needles for the ribbing

In a few of the patterns, the instructions call for the stitches to be arranged in a certain way before knitting the cuff and then rearranged when knitting the body of the mitten. It's always best to start each needle with a knit stitch. This keeps your work firm and even, and if you put the knitting down at the end of a needle, you'll always start next time with a knit stitch. If there are two knit stitches in the ribbing, always start the needle with the first knit stitch.

There is another reason for starting each needle with the same kind of stitch if possible. When knitting, you'll develop a rhythm, and before you know it, your hands will start to remember the movements. That makes knitting more enjoyable, and you'll knit faster without even needing to think about it.

STRANDED COLORWORK

Most of the mittens in the book are knitted with stranded colorwork. It's good to keep few things in mind when knitting with two colors.

GAUGE

Many knitters work stranded colorwork more tightly than stocking stitch in one color, and therefore may want to knit more loosely or use needles a half size larger than indicated for the stranded colorwork sections of the mittens.

DOMINANT AND NON-DOMINANT COLORS

The way the colors are stranded on the WS of the knitting will have an effect on which color is more dominant or obvious on the RS. Usually the main color is non-dominant and the contrasting color is dominant. To control this, the colors should be held in a certain way:

Place the **dominant color** over the index finger of your left hand, under the middle and ring fingers, and over the little finger, and hold it nearer to you. Place the **non-dominant color** over your index and middle fingers, under your ring finger, and over your little finger, keeping it farther from you. Both lengths of wool should lie between the ring finger and the little finger to hold them firm and to even the gauge.

When this method is used, both the yarns stay in place, which makes it easier to pick up the right color for the next stitch. When you get used to this method, you will eventually knit faster as well.

FINISHING OFF THE TOP OF THE MITTEN AND THE TOP OF THE THUMB

PULLING THE STITCHES TOGETHER After the decreases are done at the top of the mitten or the thumb, a few stitches will remain on the needles. Cut the yarn so the end is 4–6 in/10–15 cm; then, using a tapestry needle, thread this end through all the stitches on the needles twice. Push the needle through to the wrong side and finish off.

SLIP-STITCH METHOD Another method is to knit 1 stitch and then place it back on the left-hand needle. Slip all the stitches on the left-hand needle over the first, one by one. Thread the yarn through the last stitch. Finish off on the wrong side.

GRAFTING STITCHES TOGETHER Where the mitten ends horizontally, rather than in a point, the stitches can be grafted together with Kitchener stitch to finish the top of the mitten.

BIND OFF ON THE WRONG SIDE WITH 3-NEEDLE BIND-OFF

Where the mittens end horizontally, rather than in a point, the top of the mitten can be closed by binding off on the wrong side with the 3-needle bind-off method.

INCREASING

In the patterns in the book, various increase methods are used—for instance, where the mitten body needs to be increased after the completion of the cuff, either for greater width or to accomodate the two-color pattern.

Slanted increases are useful in creating almost invisible increases:

MAKE 1 LEFT

M1L by picking up the bar between the last stitch you knitted and the one you are about to knit, inserting the needle from front to back. Then knit into the back of this stitch. One stitch increased.

MAKE 1 RIGHT

M1R by picking up the bar between the last stitch you knitted and the one you are about to knit, inserting the needle from back to front. Then knit into the front of this stitch. One stitch increased.

M1R and M1L are often worked in pairs on either side of a thumb gusset.

KNIT TWICE IN THE SAME STITCH

kfb Increase by knitting twice into the same stitch. First, through the front as in a knit stitch; then, without slipping it off the left needle, into the back of the stitch, and then slip it off the needle. One stitch increased.

KNIT THREE TIMES IN THE SAME STITCH

kfbf Increase by knitting three times into the same stitch. First, through the front as in a knit stitch; then, without slipping it off the left needle, into the back of the stitch; and finally, through the front again, and then slip it off the needle. Two stitches increased.

YARN-OVER INCREASE

YO To work a yarn-over, bring the yarn over the right hand needle from front to back, and then into position to work the next stitch. This creates a hole and a new stitch, and is used in lace knitting. A decrease, i.e. two stitches knit together, is often paired with this increase to keep the number of stitches the same over the round. On the next round, the YO is worked as any other stitch.

DECREASING

RIGHT-LEANING DECREASE

k2tog Knit two stitches together by knitting them both *at the same time*. One stitch decreased.

LEFT-LEANING DECREASE

ssk Slip 2 stitches knitwise one at a time. Insert the left needle through both stitches in front of the right needle and knit them together through the back loop. Neither stitch is twisted and one stitch is decreased.

SL1, K2TOG, PSSO

Sl1, k2tog, psso Slip one stitch knitwise, knit the next 2 stitches together, then pass the slipped stitch over the 2 knit-together stitches. The right stitch will be on top. Two stitches decreased.

SL2TOG, K1, P2SSO

Sl2tog, k1, p2sso Slip 2 stitches knitwise *at the same time*, knit one, then pass the slipped stitches over. The middle stitch will be on top. Two stitches decreased.

WASH AND BLOCK

Run lukewarm water—no more than 90°F/30°C—into a bowl or sink with mild wool soap. Place the mittens in the water for 10–20 minutes until they are totally soaked. Let the water run off and rinse as necessary. Gently squeeze out the excess water, place the mittens on a towel, and roll the towel up. Get as much water out as possible without twisting the mittens.

Lay them out to dry where there is good air circulation. Pat them out with the palms of your hand to even out the stitches and to get the right size.

Videos with different demonstrations of the various methods and instructions for knitting the mittens in this book can be found on the website: reykjavikknittingcompany.com.

BJÖRK

These mittens are in the collection in Halldórustofa in the Textile Museum, but it is not known who knitted them originally. They are knitted in a brown main color, with a pale grey contrasting color for the pattern. The popular eight-petal rose pattern has been used in Icelandic mittens for many years in numerous variations. These mittens are an interesting example of a thumb gusset and thumb from the edge. The pattern is easy to memorize and knit.

SIZE	Women's medium
FINISHED MEASUREMENTS	11 in/27.5 cm long (incl. 2.75 in/7.5 cm ribbed cuff) and 7.5 in/19 cm around palm circumference.
YARN	CYCA #1 (sock/fingering/baby) *Pirkkalanka Ohut* (100% wool, 437 yd/400 m / 100 g) Main color (MC): blackish brown, 50 g. Contrasting color (CC): light grey, 50 g. CYCA #1 (sock/fingering/baby) *Rowan Fine Tweed* (100% wool, 98 yd/90 m / 25 g) Main color (MC): dark grey, 50 g. Contrasting color (CC): yellow, 50 g. Or similar fingering weight wool.
NEEDLES	Size US 0/2 mm set of 5 DPNs for the cuff. Size US 1/2.5 mm set of 5 DPNs for the hand. Adjust needle size if necessary to obtain the correct gauge.
OTHER MATERIALS	Scrap yarn and tapestry needle.
GAUGE	36 stitches and 36 rounds in stranded colorwork, on larger needles, after blocking = 4 in/10 cm. If the gauge is not correct, the mittens might not fit properly.
PATTERN NOTES	• See the section beginning on page 30 for special techniques concerning yarn dominance, decreasing, increasing, and finishing. • All stitches are knit stitches unless specifically noted otherwise. • Read all chart rounds from right to left. • The palm is knitted first on the right mitten, the back is knitted first on the left mitten. • The thumb is knitted on the side of these mittens. The beginning of the chart for the thumb gusset is marked with a red line. • New stitches are cast on behind the thumb gusset.

RIGHT MITTEN CUFF

With smaller needles and MC, cast on 60 stitches. Arrange stitches on the needles: 15+15+15+15 stitches and join into round.

Work in twisted rib: K5tbl (knit in the back leg of each stitch), p5, repeat for the whole round.

Work 28 rounds or about 2.75 in/7 cm.

HAND

Change to larger needles.

Round 29, inc. round: [K14, kfb] x 4 = 64 stitches.**

Begin increasing for the thumb gusset at the beginning of the next round (red line). The first 2 thumb gusset stitches are on the red line on the chart. From that point a thumb gusset chart is followed. *At the same time*, knit the pattern on the hand, first the palm and then the back.

THUMB GUSSET

Work the pattern from the chart and the increases for the thumb gusset *at the same time*.

Round 30: Kfbf, k63 = 66 stitches.

Round 31 and every odd round of the thumb gusset: Knit.

Round 32: M1R, k2, M1L, k64 = 68 stitches.

Round 34: M1R, k4, M1L, k64 = 70 stitches.

Round 36: M1R, k6, M1L, k64 = 72 stitches.

Round 38: M1R, k8, M1L, k64 = 74 stitches.

Round 40: M1R, k10, M1L, k64 = 76 stitches.

Round 42: M1R, k12, M1L, k64 = 78 stitches.

Round 44: M1R, k14, M1L, k64 = 80 stitches.

Round 46: M1R, k16, M1L, k64 = 82 stitches.

Round 48: M1R, k18, M1L, k64 = 84 stitches.

Round 50: M1R, k20, M1L, k64 = 86 stitches.

Round 51: Knit.

Place the 22 stitches of the thumb gusset onto scrap yarn. Cast on 8 stitches at the back of the thumb (green line on the chart) = 72 stitches.

Work in pattern from the chart to round 83.

START DECREASE ROUNDS

Work in pattern from the chart while working decreases. Decrease on every round on the palm side, and on alternate rounds 4 times, then decrease every round on the back.

Round 83: K1, ssk, k34, k2tog, k2, ssk, k26, k2tog, k1 = 68 stitches.

Round 84: K1, ssk, k32, k2tog, k31 = 66 stitches.

Round 85: K1, ssk, k30, k2tog, k2, ssk, k24, k2tog, k1 = 62 stitches.

Round 86: K1, ssk, k28, k2tog, k29 = 60 stitches.

Round 87: K1, ssk, k26, k2tog, k2, ssk, k22, k2tog, k1 = 56 stitches.

Round 88: K1, ssk, k24, k2tog, k27 = 54 stitches.

Round 89: K1, ssk, k22, k2tog, k2, ssk, k20, k2tog, k1 = 50 stitches.

Round 90: K1, ssk, k20, k2tog, k25 = 48 stitches.

Round 91: [K1, ssk, k18, k2tog, k1] x 2 = 44 stitches.

Round 92: [K1, ssk, k16, k2tog, k1] x 2 = 40 stitches.

Round 93: [K1, ssk, k14, k2tog, k1] x 2 = 36 stitches.

Round 94: [K1, ssk, k12, k2tog, k1] x 2 = 32 stitches.

Round 95: [K1, ssk, k10, k2tog, k1] x 2 = 28 stitches.

Round 96: [K1, ssk, k8, k2tog, k1] x 2 = 24 stitches.

Round 97: [K1, ssk, k6, k2tog, k1] x 2 = 20 stitches.

Round 98: [K1, ssk, k4, k2tog, k1] x 2 = 16 stitches.

Round 99: [K1, ssk, k2, k2tog, k1] x 2 = 12 stitches.

Close the top of the mitten (see the section about finishing, page 31).

LEFT MITTEN

Work as right mitten to **.

Begin increasing for the thumb gusset at the end of the next round (red line). The first 2 thumb gusset stitches are on the red line on the chart. From that point a thumb gusset chart is followed. *At the same time*, knit the pattern on the hand, first the back and then the palm.

THUMB GUSSET

Work the pattern from the chart and the increases for the thumb gusset *at the same time.*

Round 30: K63, kfbf = 66 stitches.

Round 31 and every odd round of the thumb gusset: Knit.

Round 32: K64, M1R, k2, M1L = 68 stitches.

Round 34: K64, M1R, k4, M1L = 70 stitches.

Round 36: K64, M1R, k6, M1L = 72 stitches.

Round 38: K64, M1R, k8, M1L = 74 stitches.

Round 40: K64, M1R, k10, M1L = 76 stitches.

Round 42: K64, M1R, k12, M1L = 78 stitches.

Round 44: K64, M1R, k14, M1L = 80 stitches.

Round 46: K64, M1R, k16, M1L = 82 stitches.

Round 48: K64, M1R, k18, M1L = 84 stitches.

Round 50: K64, M1R, k20, M1L = 86 stitches.

Round 51: Knit.

Place the 22 stitches of the thumb gusset onto scrap yarn. Cast on 8 stitches at the back of the thumb (green line on the chart) = 72 stitches.

Work in pattern from the chart to round 83.

START DECREASE ROUNDS

Work in pattern from the chart while working decreases. Decrease on every round on the palm side, and on alternate rounds 4 times, then decrease every round on the back.

Round 83: K1, ssk, k26, k2tog, k2, ssk, k34, k2tog, k1 = 68 stitches.

Round 84: K31, ssk, k32, k2tog, k1 = 66 stitches.

Round 85: K1, ssk, k24, k2tog, k2, ssk, k30, k2tog, k1 = 62 stitches.

Round 86: K29, ssk, k28, k2tog, k1 = 60 stitches.

Round 87: K1, ssk, k22, k2tog, k2, ssk, k26, k2tog, k1 = 56 stitches.

Round 88: K27, ssk, k24, k2tog, k1 = 54 stitches.

Round 89: K1, ssk, k20, k2tog, k2, ssk, k22, k2tog, k1 = 50 stitches.

Round 90: K25, ssk, k20, k2tog, k1 = 48 stitches.

Round 91: [K1, ssk, k18, k2tog, k1] x 2 = 44 stitches.

Round 92: [K1, ssk, k16, k2tog, k1] x 2 = 40 stitches.

Round 93: [K1, ssk, k14, k2tog, k1] x 2 = 36 stitches.

Round 94: [K1, ssk, k12, k2tog, k1] x 2 = 32 stitches.

Round 95: [K1, ssk, k10, k2tog, k1] x 2 = 28 stitches.

Round 96: [K1, ssk, k8, k2tog, k1] x 2 = 24 stitches.

Round 97: [K1, ssk, k6, k2tog, k1] x 2 = 20 stitches.

Round 98: [K1, ssk, k4, k2tog, k1] x 2 = 16 stitches.

Round 99: [K1, ssk, k2, k2tog, k1] x 2 = 12 stitches.

Close the top of the mitten (see the section about finishing, page 31).

THUMB (BOTH MITTENS)

Place the 22 stitches of the thumb gusset on 2 DPNs. Pick up and knit 10 stitches at the back of the gusset (purple line on the chart) = 32 stitches. Work in pattern from the chart and start decreasing on round 17.

Round 17: Ssk, k8, [ssk, k9] x 2 = 29 stitches.

Round 18: Ssk, k7, [ssk, k8] x 2 = 26 stitches.

Round 19: Ssk, k6, [ssk, k7] x 2 = 23 stitches.

Round 20: Ssk, k5, [ssk, k6] x 2 = 20 stitches.

Round 21: Ssk, k4, [ssk, k5] x 2 = 17 stitches.

Round 22: Ssk, k3, [ssk, k4] x 2 = 14 stitches.

Round 23: Ssk, k2, [ssk, k3] x 2 = 11 stitches.

Round 24: Ssk, k1, [ssk, k2] x 2 = 8 stitches.

Round 25: Ssk, [ssk, k1] x 2 = 5 stitches.

Close the top of the thumb in the same way as the top of the mitten.

FINISHING

Weave in all ends. Wash and block both mittens, patting them gently to get the right size and to even out the stitches.

Left mitten

Right mitten

Thumb gusset and thumb

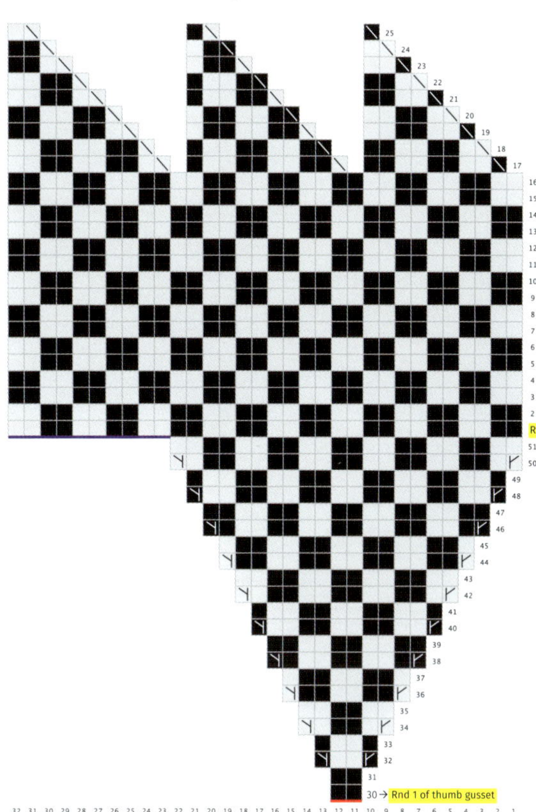
Rnd 1 of thumb
30 → Rnd 1 of thumb gusset

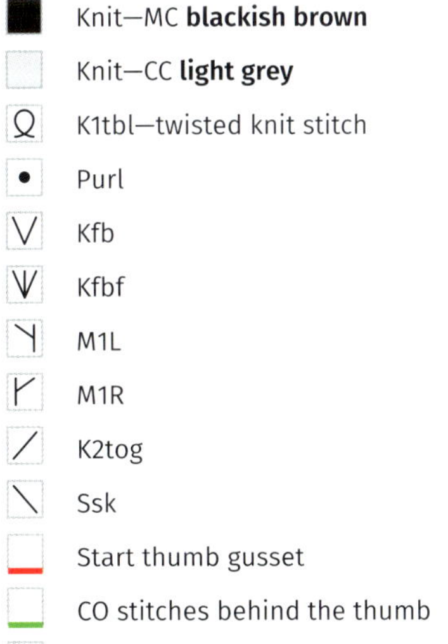
Knit—MC **blackish brown**
Knit—CC **light grey**
K1tbl—twisted knit stitch
Purl
Kfb
Kfbf
M1L
M1R
K2tog
Ssk
Start thumb gusset
CO stitches behind the thumb
Start knitting behind the thumb

LÁRA

In the knitted pattern of these mittens we can clearly see the lines of feathers drawn with knitted stitches. The original mittens are from Halldórustofa, where they are first described in 1961 as originating from the district of Múlasýsla and are considered unusual for mittens from the east coast. Headmistress Sigrún Blöndal (1883–1944) taught her students at Hallormsstaður Women's Domestic College to knit these mittens. They are knitted with greyish brown and white 2-ply yarn. The cuff is knitted in a traditional wave-like lace pattern. The lace pattern continues up the body of the mitten in alternate light and dark rounds. This technique creates mittens that are both interesting and unusual.

SIZE Women's medium

FINISHED MEASUREMENTS 11 in/27 cm (incl. 3 in/8 cm cuff) and 7.5 in/19 cm around palm circumference

YARN CYCA #1 (sock/fingering/baby) *Pirkkalanka Ohut* (100% wool, 437 yd/400 m / 100 g) Main color (MC): reddish brown, 50 g. Contrasting color (CC): white, 50 g.

CYCA #1 (sock/fingering/baby) *Rowan Fine Tweed* (100% wool, 98 yd/90 m / 25 g) Main color (MC): dark sea green, 50 g. Contrasting color (CC): light blue, 25 g.

Or similar fingering weight wool.

NEEDLES Size US 0/2 mm set of 5 DPNs for the cuff. Size US 1/2.5 mm set of 5 DPNs for the hand. Adjust needle size if necessary to obtain the correct gauge.

OTHER MATERIALS Scrap yarn and tapestry needle.

GAUGE Cuff: 36 stitches and 36 rows in lace pattern, on smaller needles, after blocking = 4 in/10 cm.

Hand: 40 stitches and 30 rounds in stranded colorwork, on larger needles, after blocking = 4 in/10 cm.

If the gauge is not correct, the mittens might not fit properly.

PATTERN NOTES

- See the section beginning on page 30 for special techniques concerning yarn dominance, decreasing, increasing, and finishing.
- All stitches are knit stitches unless specifically noted otherwise.
- Both mittens are knitted from the same chart.
- The chart is read from right to left.
- The palm is knitted first on the right mitten, and the back of the hand is knitted first on the left mitten.
- The thumb opening is knit at the beginning of the round on the right mitten and at the end of the round on the left mitten.
- Note that the pattern chart shows the yarn colors in the order used for each round, but the stitches create diagonal stripes in CC (increases) pointing up from the vertical column.

- When knitting this type of pattern, the beginning of the round moves one stitch to the left on every increase/decrease round (every second round). To manage this, you slip the first stitch and move it to the end of the round (to the right needle). This stitch is included in the chart as the last stitch of the round.

CUFF

With smaller needles and MC, cast on 72 stitches. Arrange on 4 DPNs: 18+18+18+18 stitches and join into round. Move stitches between needles as needed.

Work the cuff in pattern with decreases and increases, *at the same time* changing colors for the stripes: 3 rounds MC, 2 rounds CC, 2 rounds MC, 3 rounds CC, 2 rounds MC, 2 rounds CC and 6 rounds MC.

Round 1: Knit.

Round 2: [K7, yo, k1, yo, k7, sl2tog, k1, p2sso] x 4.

Rounds 3: Knit.

Round 4: Slip the first stitch and move it to the right needle (end of round). Work [k7, yo, k1, yo, k7, sl2tog, k1, p2sso] x 4.

Rounds 5–30: Repeat rounds 3–4.

HAND

Change to larger needles and work every stitch alternately with MC and CC for the whole hand (see chart). Make sure to pay attention to yarn dominance.

At the same time, knit in pattern:

Round 31: Knit.

Round 32: Slip the first stitch and move it to the right needle (end of round). Work [K7, M1R, k1, M1L, k7, sl2tog, k1, p2sso] x 4.

Rounds 33–44: Repeat rounds 31–32, following the chart for color changes.

THUMB OPENING

Round 45:

RIGHT MITTEN

Knit 2, knit 13 with scrap yarn (the purple line on the chart). Slip these stitches back onto the left hand needle, then work in pattern to the end of the round.

LEFT MITTEN

Work in pattern until there are 16 stitches left in the round. Knit the next 13 stitches with scrap yarn (red line on chart). Slip these 13 stitches back onto the left hand needle, then work in pattern to the end of the round.

Work round 32 once more, following the chart for color changes.

Repeat rounds 31–32, following the chart for color changes, until the first decrease round is reached, round 85.

Continue in pattern while decreasing.

8 stitches are decreased on every round in the same place as the decreases are made in the cuff and hand, but now on every round. No more increases are worked in the pattern from here on.

Round 85: Slip the first stitch and move it to the right needle (end of round). Work [k15, sl2tog, k1, p2sso] x 4 = 64 stitches.

Round 86: Slip the first stitch and move it to the right needle (end of round). Work [k13, sl2tog, k1, p2sso] x 4 = 56 stitches

Round 87: Slip the first stitch and move it to the right needle (end of round). Work [k11, sl2tog, k1, p2sso] x 4 = 48 stitches

Round 88: Slip the first stitch and move it to the right needle (end of round). Work [k9, sl2tog, k1, p2sso] x 4 = 40 stitches.

Round 89: Slip the first stitch and move it to the right needle (end of round). Work [k7, sl2tog, k1, p2sso] x 4 = 32 stitches.

Round 90: Slip the first stitch and move it to the right needle (end of round). Work [k5, sl2tog, k1, p2sso] x 4 = 24 stitches.

Round 91: Slip the first stitch and move it to the right needle (end of round). Work [k3, sl2tog, k1, p2sso] x 4 = 16 stitches.

Round 92: Slip the first stitch and move it to the right needle (end of round). Work [k1, sl2tog, k1, p2sso] x 4 = 8 stitches.

Close the top of the mitten (see the section about finishing, page 31).

THUMB

Divide the stitches from the scrap yarn onto 3 DPNs (see the section about thumbs, page 22).

Pick up and knit 1 stitch on either side of the opening, and one extra stitch in the middle at the top of the opening = 28 thumb stitches.

Work the same pattern for the thumb and make sure it aligns with the pattern on the body (see chart). Work until the 21st round is reached.

Round 1: Knit.

Round 2: Slip the first stitch and move it to the right needle (end of round). Work [k5, M1R, k1, M1L, k5, sl2tog, k1, p2sso] x 2.

Rounds 3–20: Repeat rounds 1–2.

DECREASES

Decrease in the same way as for the top of the mitten, 4 stitches each round:

Round 21: Slip the first stitch and move it to the right needle (end of round). Work [k11, sl2tog, k1, p2sso] x 2 = 24 stitches.

Round 22: Slip the first stitch and move it to the right needle (end of round). Work [k9, sl2tog, k1, p2sso] x 2 = 20 stitches.

Round 23: Slip the first stitch and move it to the right needle (end of round). Work [k7, sl2tog, k1, p2sso] x 2 = 16 stitches.

Round 24: Slip the first stitch and move it to the right needle (end of round). Work [k5, sl2tog, k1, p2sso] x 2 = 12 stitches.

Round 25: Slip the first stitch and move it to the right needle (end of round). Work [k3, sl2tog, k1, p2sso] x 2 = 8 stitches.

Close the top of the thumb in the same way as the top of the mitten.

FINISHING

Weave in all ends. Wash and block both mittens, patting them gently to get the right size and to even out the stitches.

Left and right mittens

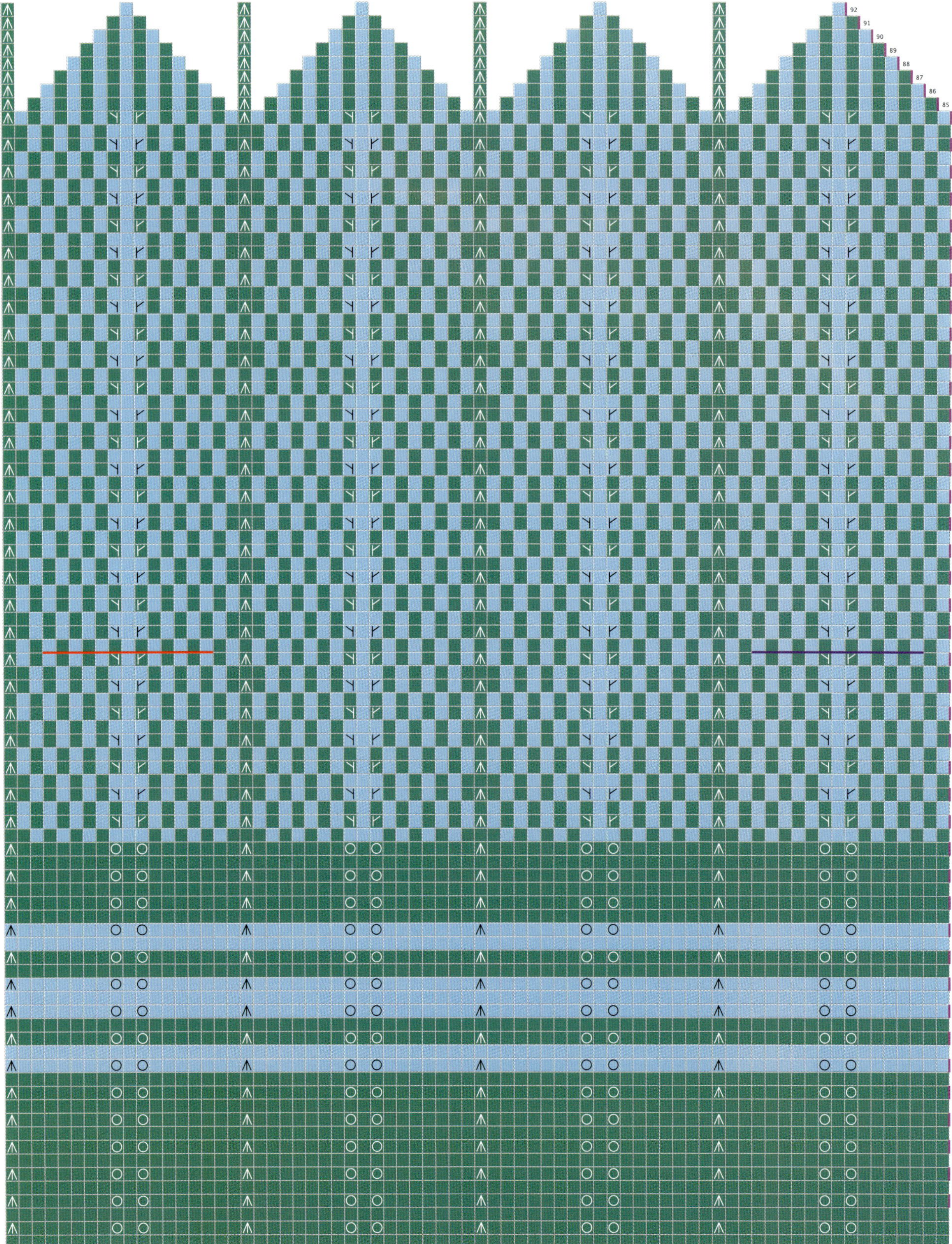

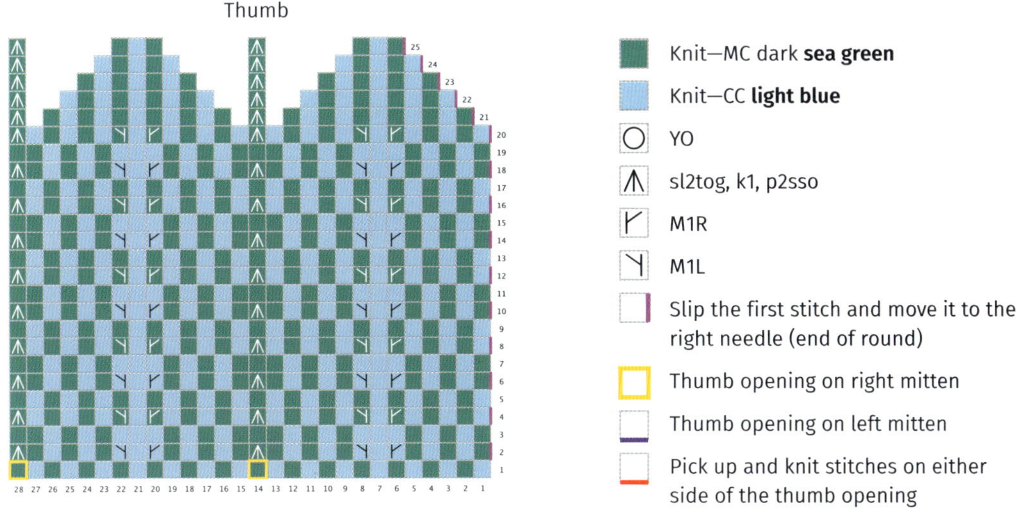
Thumb
Knit—MC dark **sea green**
Knit—CC **light blue**
YO
sl2tog, k1, p2sso
M1R
M1L
Slip the first stitch and move it to the right needle (end of round)
Thumb opening on right mitten
Thumb opening on left mitten
Pick up and knit stitches on either side of the thumb opening

ERLA

These lace mittens were knitted by Sveinbjörg Brynjólfsdóttir from Stóri-Dalur (1883–1966) and were donated to the Textile Museum in 1988. Knitting instructions for them have appeared before in the book *Mittens* by Kristín Harðardóttir, and they have always been very popular. The cuff and back of the mittens are worked in a shell pattern. The palm is knitted in stocking stitch, and the thumb extends with a gusset from the side of the mittens. These mittens are an enjoyable project for experienced knitters who want to try a lace pattern.

SIZE	Women's medium. Be aware that the lace pattern on the back of the mittens is a bit stretchy.
FINISHED MEASUREMENTS	10.5 in/26 cm long (incl. 2 in/5 cm ribbed cuff) and 6.5 in/16 cm around palm circumference.
YARN	CYCA #1 (sock/fingering/baby) *Pirkkalanka Ohut* (100% wool, 437 yd/400 m / 100 g) Light brown, 50 g. CYCA #2 (sport/baby) *Mohair by Canard Kid Mohair 2-ply* (65% Mohair, 35% Merino, 193 yd/176 m / 50 g) Curry, 100 g. Or similar fingering weight wool.
NEEDLES	Size US 0/2 mm set of 5 DPNs. Adjust needle size if necessary to obtain the correct gauge.
OTHER MATERIALS	2 stitch markers, scrap yarn, and tapestry needle.
GAUGE	34 stitches and 44 rounds in shell pattern, after blocking = 4 in/10 cm. If the gauge is not correct, the mittens might not fit properly.

PATTERN NOTES

- See the section beginning on page 30 for special techniques concerning yarn dominance, decreasing, increasing, and finishing.
- All stitches are knit stitches unless specifically noted otherwise.
- The back of the hand is knitted first on the right mitten, followed by the palm. The palm is knitted first followed, by the back of the hand on the left mitten.
- Read all chart rounds from right to left.
- These mittens have a thumb gusset and an inner gusset behind the thumb which ends after the 68th round (marked with a purple line).
- The mittens can be finished at the top either by grafting the stitches together or by binding off on the wrong side with a 3-needle bind-off.

Right mitten

Thumb gusset and thumb

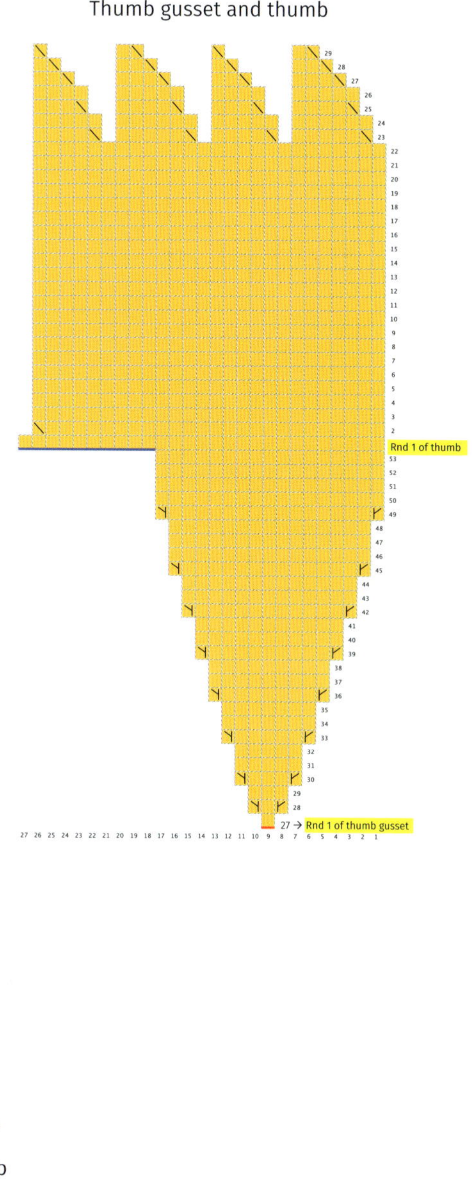

Gusset behind thumb

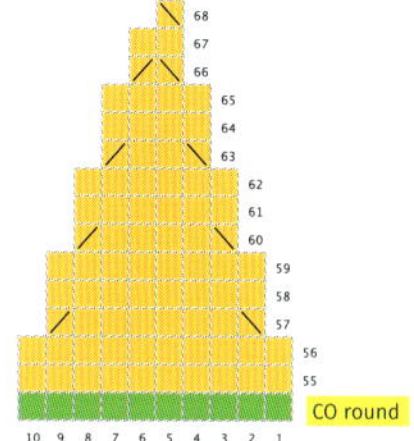

- Knit
- Purl
- YO
- Ssk
- Sl1, k1, psso
- K2tog
- M1R
- M1L
- Start thumb gusset
- CO stitches behind the thumb
- Start gusset behind the thumb
- End gusset behind the thumb

HILDUR

These patterned mittens were knitted by Guðrún Bjarnadóttir from Holtastaðakot (1930–2009) and were donated to the Textile Museum in 1980. Traditional pattern elements from the West Fjords are very much evident here: a pale background and a colorful patterned band at the top and bottom of the mitten. The ribbing on the cuff is broken up with a colorful border. Stitches for the thumb are picked up after the body of the mitten is knitted. As with all stranded knitting, the gauge is very important and these mittens are great to practice on.

SIZE Women's medium

FINISHED MEASUREMENTS 10 in/25 cm long (incl. 2.5 in/6 cm cuff) and 7.5 in/19 cm around palm circumference.

YARN CYCA #1 (sock/fingering/baby) *Pirkkalanka Ohut* (100% wool, 437 yd/400 m / 100 g) Main color (MC): light brown, 50 g. Contrasting colors (CC): red, yellow, green, black, purple, sky blue, 25 g of each.

CYCA #1 (sock/fingering/baby) *Rowan Fine Tweed* (100% wool, 98 yd/90 m / 25 g) Main color (MC): black, 50 g. Contrasting colors (CC): light grey, yellow, dark grey, light green, mustard, dark green, 25 g of each.

Or similar fingering weight wool.

NEEDLES Size US 0/2 mm set of 5 DPNs for the cuff. Size US 1/2.5 mm set of 5 DPNs for the hand. Adjust needle size if necessary to obtain the correct gauge.

OTHER MATERIALS Scrap yarn and tapestry needle.

GAUGE 36 stitches and 40 rounds in stocking stitch, on larger needles, after blocking = 4 in/10 cm.

36 stitches and 42 rounds in stranded colorwork, on larger needles, after blocking = 4 in/10 cm.

If the gauge is not correct, the mittens might not fit properly.

PATTERN NOTES

- See the section beginning on page 30 for special techniques concerning yarn dominance, decreasing, increasing, and finishing.
- All stitches are knit stitches unless specifically noted otherwise.
- Both mittens are knitted from the same chart.
- Read all chart rounds from right to left.
- The thumb is worked at the beginning of the round on the right mitten and at the end of the round on the left mitten.

- Some knitters knit tighter when knitting stranded colorwork. So it may be necessary to change needle sizes between single-color and stranded knitting in order to maintain gauge.

CUFF

With smaller needles and MC, cast on 66 stitches using the long-tail cast-on (see the section about cast-ons, page 28, for other methods). Arrange stitches on the needles: 15 + 18 + 15 + 18 stitches and join into round. Work 8 rounds of ribbing: k2, p1. Work the next 9 rounds from the chart.

Then work the next 7 rounds with MC in ribbing: k2, p1.

HAND

Change to larger needles.

Round 25, inc. round: [K11, M1L] x 6 = 72 stitches.

Rearrange stitches so there are 18 stitches on each of the four needles. Work in pattern from the chart to round 53.

Round 53: Work in pattern from the chart while working thumb openings:

RIGHT MITTEN

K2, k12 stitches with scrap yarn (yellow line on the chart), slip these 12 stitches back onto left needle and knit in pattern to the end of the round.

LEFT MITTEN

Knit until 14 stitches are left in the round. K12 stitches with scrap yarn (red line on the chart), slip these 12 stitches back onto left needle and knit in pattern to the end of the round.

BOTH MITTENS

Work in pattern from the chart to round 91.

START DECREASE ROUNDS

Work in pattern from the chart while working decreases.

Decrease 4 stitches on the indicated rounds as follows:

Round 91: [Ssk, k32, k2tog] x 2 = 68 stitches.

Rounds 92, 94, 96, 98, and 100: Knit.

Round 93: [Ssk, k30, k2tog] x 2 = 64 stitches.

Round 95: [Ssk, k28, k2tog] x 2 = 60 stitches.

Round 97: [Ssk, k26, k2tog] x 2 = 56 stitches.

Round 99: [Ssk, k24, k2tog] x 2 = 52 stitches.

Round 101: [Ssk, k22, k2tog] x 2 = 48 stitches.

Round 102: [Ssk, k20, k2tog] x 2 = 44 stitches.

Round 103: [Ssk, k18, k2tog] x 2 = 40 stitches.

Round 104: [Ssk, k16, k2tog] x 2 = 36 stitches.

Round 105: [Ssk, k14, k2tog] x 2 = 32 stitches.

Round 106: [Ssk, k12, k2tog] x 2 = 28 stitches.

Round 107: [Ssk, k10, k2tog] x 2 = 24 stitches.

Round 108: [Ssk, k8, k2tog] x 2 = 20 stitches.

Round 109: [Ssk, k6, k2tog] x 2 = 16 stitches.

Round 110: [Ssk, k4, k2tog] x 2 = 12 stitches.

Round 111: [Ssk, k2, k2tog] x 2 = 8 stitches.

Close the top of the mitten (see the section about finishing, page 31).

THUMB

Remove scrap yarn, place stitches on 3 needles, work round with MC, picking up 2 stitches on either side of the opening and one extra stitch at the top of the opening = 28 stitches. Work in pattern from the chart and start decreasing on round 19.

Round 19: [Ssk, k5] x 4 = 24 stitches.

Rounds 20, 22, and 24: Knit.

Round 21: [Ssk, k4] x 4 = 20 stitches.

Round 23: [Ssk, k3] x 4 = 16 stitches.

Round 25: [Ssk, k2] x 4 = 12 stitches.

Round 26: [Ssk, k1] x 4 = 8 stitches.

Round 27: [Ssk] x 4 = 4 stitches.

Close the top of the thumb in the same way as the top of the mitten.

FINISHING Weave in all ends. Wash and block both mittens, patting them gently to get the right size and to even out the stitches.

Left and right mittens

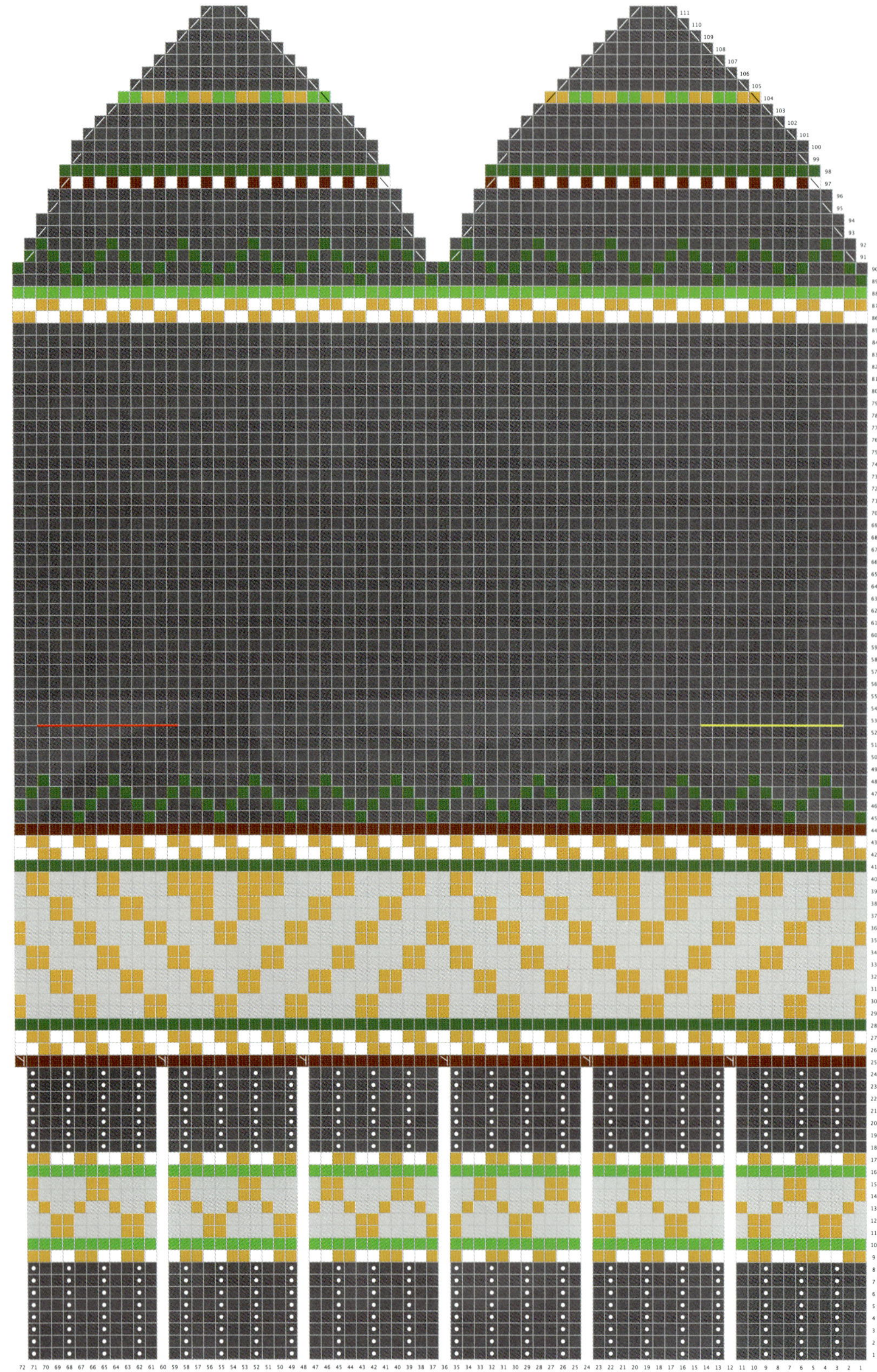

Thumb

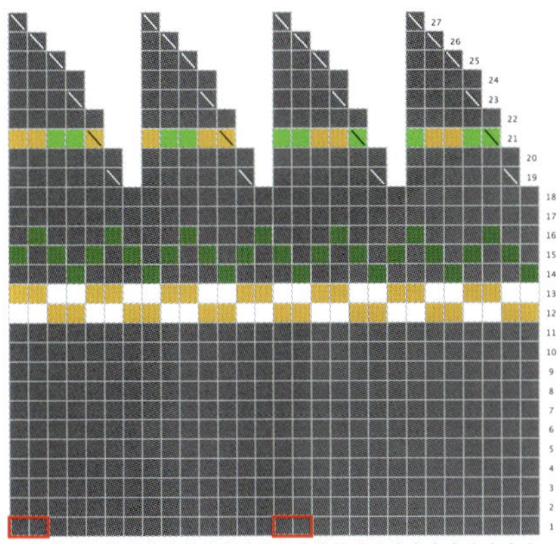

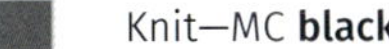
Knit—MC **black**

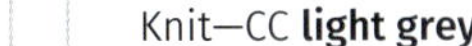
Knit—CC **light grey**

Knit—CC **yellow**

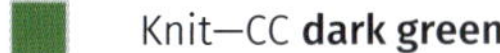
Knit—CC **dark green**

Knit—CC **light green**

Knit—CC **mustard**

Knit—CC **dark grey**

Purl

M1L

K2tog

Ssk

Thumb opening on right mitten

Thumb opening on left mitten

Pick up and knit stitches on either side of the thumb opening

VALA

These stranded mittens knitted in brown and white wool are from Halldórustofa in the Textile Museum. The brown cuff is knitted in twisted knit stitch (knitted through the back loop). The mitten pattern consists of white vertical lines with a zigzag pattern between them. Twisted knitting is also incorporated into the body knitting. Stitches are increased after the cuff for the thumb, and a gusset is also added.

SIZE: Women's medium

FINISHED MEASUREMENTS: 10.5 in/26 cm long (incl 2.5 in/6 cm ribbed cuff) and 7 in/18 cm around palm circumference.

YARN: CYCA #1 (sock/fingering/baby) *Pirkkalanka Ohut* (100% wool, 437 yd/400 m / 100 g)
Main color (MC): dark brown, 50 g.
Contrasting color (CC): off-white, 50 g.

CYCA #1 (sock/fingering/baby) *Rowan Fine Tweed* (100% wool, 98 yd/90 m / 25 g)
Main color (MC): dark brown, 50 g.
Contrasting color (CC): turquoise, 50 g.

Or similar fingering weight wool.

NEEDLES: Size US 0/2 mm set of 5 DPNs for the cuff. Size US 1.5/2.5 mm set of 5 DPNs for the hand. Adjust needle size if necessary to obtain the correct gauge.

OTHER MATERIALS: Scrap yarn and tapestry needle.

GAUGE: 36 stitches and 36 rounds in stranded colorwork, on larger needles, after blocking = 4 in/10 cm.

If the gauge is not correct, the mittens might not fit properly.

PATTERN NOTES:

- See the section beginning on page 30 for special techniques concerning yarn dominance, decreasing, increasing, and finishing.
- The cuff is worked with alternating twisted knit stitches and purl stitches. The main part of the mitten is worked in stockinette stitch, but with a few twisted knit stitches that are worked in a column for the entire length of the mitten.
- Read all chart rounds from right to left.
- The right and left mittens are identical, and so only one chart is shown. Work two identical mittens and follow blocking instructions to create right and left mittens.
- These mittens have a thumb gusset, which begins at the red line on the main chart and then follows a thumb gusset chart.

- The stitches behind the thumb are decreased to form a gusset. The stitches are also charted.

BOTH MITTENS

CUFF

With MC and smaller needles, cast on 62 stitches. Arrange stitches on the needles: 16+16+16+14 stitches and join into round.

Work the cuff in k1tbl, p1 ribbing for 24 rounds (approximately 2.5 in/6 cm).

HAND

Change to larger needles.

Round 25, inc. round: K6, [M1L, k10] x 5, M1L, k6 = 68 stitches.

THUMB GUSSET

Work two-color stranded knitting from the chart. In the next round begin increasing for the thumb (red line on the chart). At that point follow the thumb chart, and *at the same time* the chart for the body of the mitten.

Round 26: [K1tbl, k10] x 5, k1tbl, M1R, k1, k1tbl, k10 = 69 stitches.

Rounds 27–28: [K1tbl, k10] x 5, k1tbl, k2, k1tbl, k10.

Round 29: [K1tbl, k10] x 5, k1tbl, M1R, k2, M1L, k1tbl, k10 = 71 stitches.

Round 30: [K1tbl, k10] x 5, k1tbl, M1R, k4, M1L, k1tbl, k10 = 73 stitches.

Round 31: [K1tbl, k10] x 5, k1tbl, k6, k1tbl, k10.

Round 32: [K1tbl, k10] x 5, k1tbl, M1R, k6, M1L, k1tbl, k10 = 75 stitches.

Round 33: [K1tbl, k10] x 5, k1tbl, k8, k1tbl, k10.

Round 34: [K1tbl, k10] x 5, k1tbl, M1R, k8, M1L, k1tbl, k10 = 77 stitches.

Rounds 35–37: [K1tbl, k10] x 5, k1tbl, k10, k1tbl, k10.

Round 38: [K1tbl, k10] x 5, k1tbl, M1R, k10, M1L, k1tbl, k10 = 79 stitches.

Work the next 13 rounds without increasing.

Round 52: Work in pattern to thumb gusset stitches. Place 14 thumb gusset stitches on scrap yarn. Cast on 12 stitches, which will form the inner thumb gusset behind the thumb (shown in blue on the chart), and work to the end of the round = 77 stitches.

THUMB GUSSET BEHIND THE THUMB

Work the mitten from the chart and the gusset decreases *at the same time* (separate color chart for the gusset).

Rounds 53–58: [K1tbl, k10] x 7.

Round 59: [K1tbl, k10] x 5, k1tbl, ssk, k6, k2tog, k1tbl, k10 = 75 stitches.

Round 60: [K1tbl, k10] x 5, k1tbl, k8, k1tbl, k10.

Round 61: [K1tbl, k10] x 5, k1tbl, ssk, k4, k2tog, k1tbl, k10 = 73 stitches.

Round 62: [K1tbl, k10] x 5, k1tbl, k6, k1tbl, k10.

Round 63: [K1tbl, k10] x 5, k1tbl, ssk, k2, k2tog, k1tbl, k10 = 71 stitches.

Round 64: [K1tbl, k10] x 5, k1tbl, k4, k1tbl, k10.

Round 65: [K1tbl, k10] x 5, k1tbl, ssk, k2tog, k1tbl, k10 = 69 stitches.

Round 66: [K1tbl, k10] x 5, k1tbl, ssk, k1tbl, k10 = 68 stitches.

Round 67: [K1tbl, k10] x 5, sl2tog, k1, p2sso, k10 = 66 stitches.

Rounds 68–95: [K1tbl, k10] x 6.

START DECREASE ROUNDS

Continue working from the chart while decreasing 12 stitches on each of the next 5 rounds.

Round 96: [K1tbl, k3, k2tog, ssk, k3] x 6 = 54 stitches.

Round 97: [K1tbl, k2, k2tog, ssk, k2] x 6 = 42 stitches.

Round 98: [K1tbl, k1, k2tog, ssk, k1] x 6 = 30 stitches.

Round 99: [K1tbl, k2tog, ssk] x 6 = 18 stitches.

Round 100: [Sl2, k1, p2sso] x 6 = 6 stitches.

Close the top of the mitten (see the section about finishing, page 31).

THUMB

Place the 14 thumb gusset stitches on two needles. Pick up and knit 14 stitches behind the thumb (pink line in chart) = 28 thumb stitches. Work in pattern from the chart and start decreasing on round 21.

Round 21: K1tbl, ssk, k8, k2tog, k1tbl, k1, ssk, k8, k2tog, k1 = 24 stitches.

Round 22: K1tbl, ssk, k6, k2tog, k1tbl, k1, ssk, k6, k2tog, k1 = 20 stitches.

Round 23: K1tbl, ssk, k4, k2tog, k1tbl, k1, ssk, k4, k2tog, k1 = 16 stitches.

Round 24: K1tbl, ssk, k2, k2tog, k1tbl, k1, ssk, k2, k2tog, k1 = 12 stitches.

Round 25: K1tbl, ssk, k2tog, k1tbl, k1, ssk, k2tog, k1 = 8 stitches.

Round 26: K1tbl, k2tog, k1tbl, k1, k2tog, k1 = 6 stitches.

Close the top of the thumb in the same way as the top of the mitten.

FINISHING

Weave in all ends. Wash and block both mittens, patting them gently to get the right size and to even out the stitches. As both mittens are the same, lay the right mitten flat with the thumb on the left side and the left mitten flat with the thumb on the right side. When this is done, the fold at the top of the mitten will be in the right place.

Left and right mittens

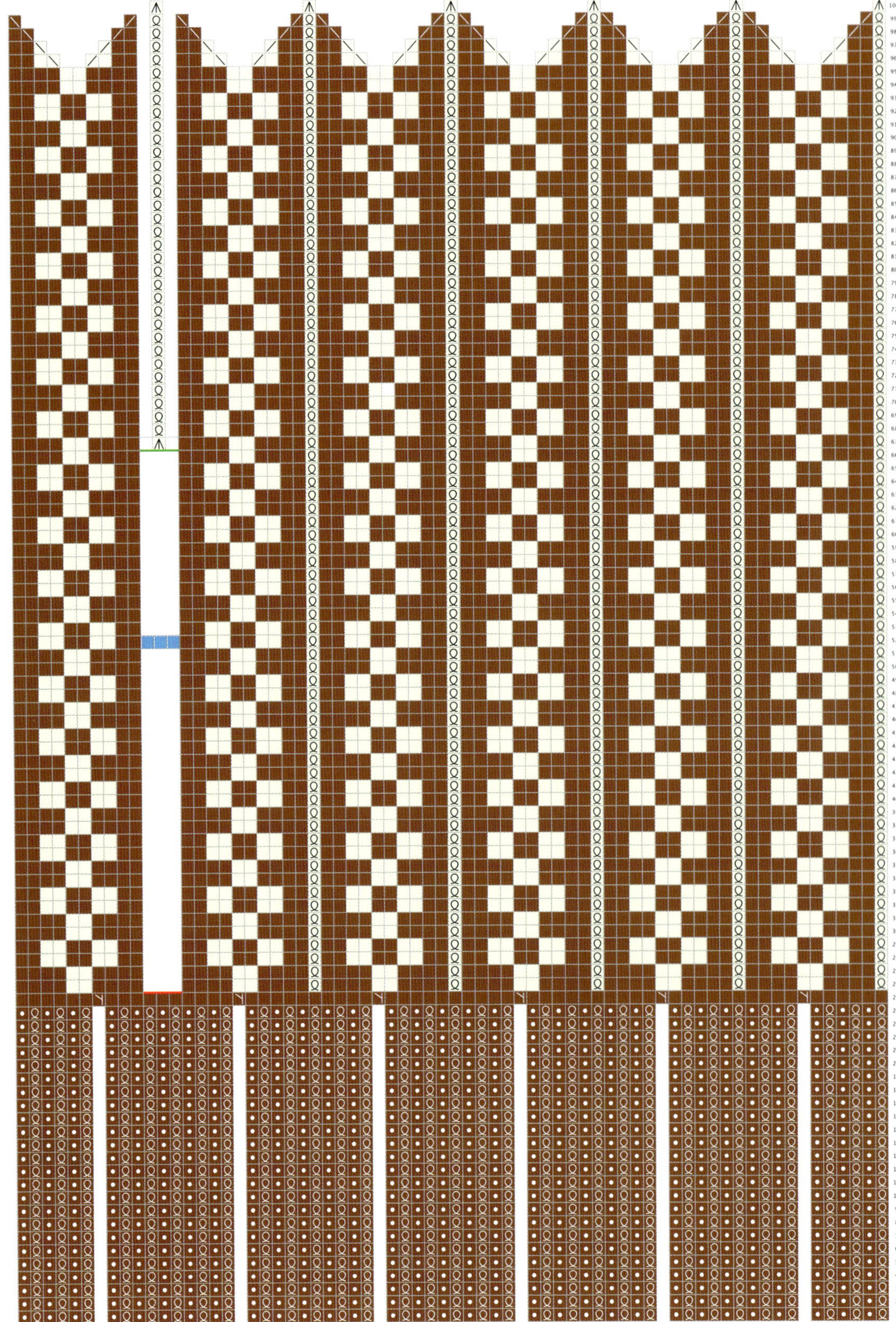

Thumb gusset and thumb

Rnd 1 of thumb

26 → Rnd 1 of thumb gusset

Gusset behind thumb

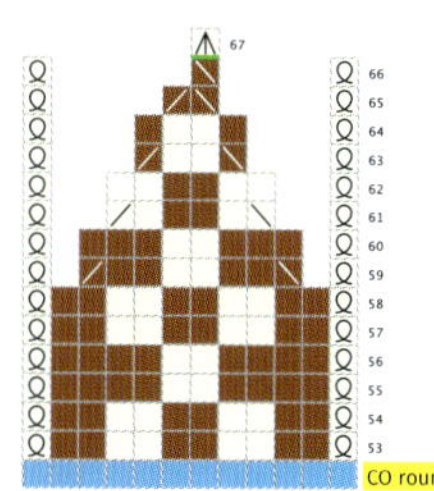

- Knit—MC **brown**
- Knit—CC **off-white**
- Purl
- K1tbl—twisted knit stitch
- M1L
- M1R
- Ssk
- K2tog
- Sl2tog, k1, p2sso
- Start thumb gusset
- Pick up and knit stitches behind the thumb
- Start gusset behind the thumb
- End gusset behind the thumb

DRÍFA

A beautiful pair of mittens from Halldórustofa. It's not known how old these mittens are, nor who knit them, but the pattern is very similar to mittens found in the book *Vefnaður- og útsaumsgerðir*, published in 1928 by the Icelandic Handcrafts Association. The main color is white and the contrast color a light brown. The cuff is unusual in that it incorporates stranded knitting in both stocking stitch and ribbing. Various patterns are knitted into the body and the thumb. Attention needs to be paid to the varying tensions for knitting in one color and in two colors. A project for experienced knitters.

SIZE Women's medium

FINISHED MEASUREMENTS 11 in/27.5 cm long (incl. 3 in/7.5 cm ribbed cuff) and 7.5 in/19 cm around palm circumference.

YARN CYCA #1 (sock/fingering/baby) *Pirkkalanka Ohut* (100% wool, 437 yd/400 m / 100 g)
Main color (MC): white, 50 g.
Contrasting color (CC): light brown, 50 g.

CYCA #1 (sock/fingering/baby) *Rowan Fine Tweed* (100% wool, 98 yd/90 m / 25 g)
Main color (MC): curry yellow, 50 g.
Contrasting color (CC): green blue, 25 g.

Or similar fingering weight wool.

NEEDLES Size US 0/2 mm set of 5 DPNs for the cuff. Size US 1/2.5 mm set of 5 DPNs for the hand. Adjust needle size if necessary to obtain the correct gauge.

OTHER MATERIALS Scrap yarn and tapestry needle.

GAUGE 34 stitches and 38 rounds in stranded colorwork, on larger needles, after blocking = 4 in/10 cm.

If the gauge is not correct, the mittens might not fit properly.

PATTERN NOTES

- See the section beginning on page 30 for special techniques concerning yarn dominance, decreasing, increasing, and finishing.
- All stitches are knit stitches unless specifically noted otherwise.
- Both mittens are knitted from the same chart.
- Read all chart rounds from right to left.
- The thumb is worked at the beginning of the round on the right mitten and at the end of the round on the left mitten.

CUFF With smaller needles and MC, cast on 64 stitches. Arrange stitches evenly on the needles and join into round.

Following the chart, begin the stranded two-color cuff with a purl round followed by alternate columns of ribbing and stocking stitch. Special care needs to be paid to color dominance (see the section on page 30).

HAND — Change to larger needles on the 25th round and begin following the chart for the stranded colorwork. Work in pattern from the chart to round 47.

Round 47: Work in pattern from the chart while working thumb openings:

RIGHT MITTEN — K1, k13 stitches with scrap yarn (green line on the chart), slip these 13 stitches back onto left needle and knit in pattern to the end of the round.

LEFT MITTEN — Knit until 14 stitches are left in the round. K13 stitches with scrap yarn (red line on the chart), slip these 13 stitches back onto left needle and knit in pattern to the end of the round.

BOTH MITTENS — Work in pattern from the chart to round 80.

START DECREASE ROUNDS — Work in pattern from the chart while working decreases. Decrease 4 stitches across the round every alternate round 7 times and then every round as follows:

Round 80: [K1, ssk, k26, k2tog, k1] x 2 = 60 stitches.

Rounds 81, 83, 85, 87, 89, 91, and 93: Knit.

Round 82: [K1, ssk, k24, k2tog, k1] x 2 = 56 stitches.

Round 84: [K1, ssk, k22, k2tog, k1] x 2 = 52 stitches.

Round 86: [K1, ssk, k20, k2tog, k1] x 2 = 48 stitches.

Round 88: [K1, ssk, k18, k2tog, k1] x 2 = 44 stitches.

Round 90: [K1, ssk, k16, k2tog, k1] x 2 = 40 stitches.

Round 92: [K1, ssk, k14, k2tog, k1] x 2 = 36 stitches.

Round 94: [K1, ssk, k12, k2tog, k1] x 2 = 32 stitches.

Round 95: [K1, ssk, k10, k2tog, k1] x 2 = 28 stitches.

Round 96: [K1, ssk, k8, k2tog, k1] x 2 = 24 stitches.

Round 97: [K1, ssk, k6, k2tog, k1] x 2 = 20 stitches.

Round 98: [K1, ssk, k4, k2tog, k1] x 2 = 16 stitches.

Round 99: [K1, ssk, k2, k2tog, k1] x 2 = 12 stitches.

Round 100: [K1, ssk, k2tog, k1] x 2 = 8 stitches.

Close the top of the mitten (see the section about finishing, page 31).

THUMB

Remove scrap yarn, place stitches on 3 needles and knit around in pattern, picking up 2 stitches on either side of the opening and one extra stitch at the top of the opening = 30 stitches. Work in pattern from the chart and start decreasing on round 25.

Round 25: [K1, ssk, k9, k2tog, k1] x 2 = 26 stitches.

Round 26: [K1, ssk, k7, k2tog, k1] x 2 = 22 stitches.

Round 27: [K1, ssk, k5, k2tog, k1] x 2 = 18 stitches.

Round 28: [K1, ssk, k3, k2tog, k1] x 2 = 14 stitches.

Round 29: [K1, ssk, k1, k2tog, k1] x 2 = 10 stitches.

Round 30: [K1, sl1, k2tog, psso, k1] x 2 = 6 stitches.

Close the top of the thumb in the same way as the top of the mitten.

FINISHING

Weave in all ends. Wash and block both mittens, patting them gently to get the right size and to even out the stitches.

Left and right mittens

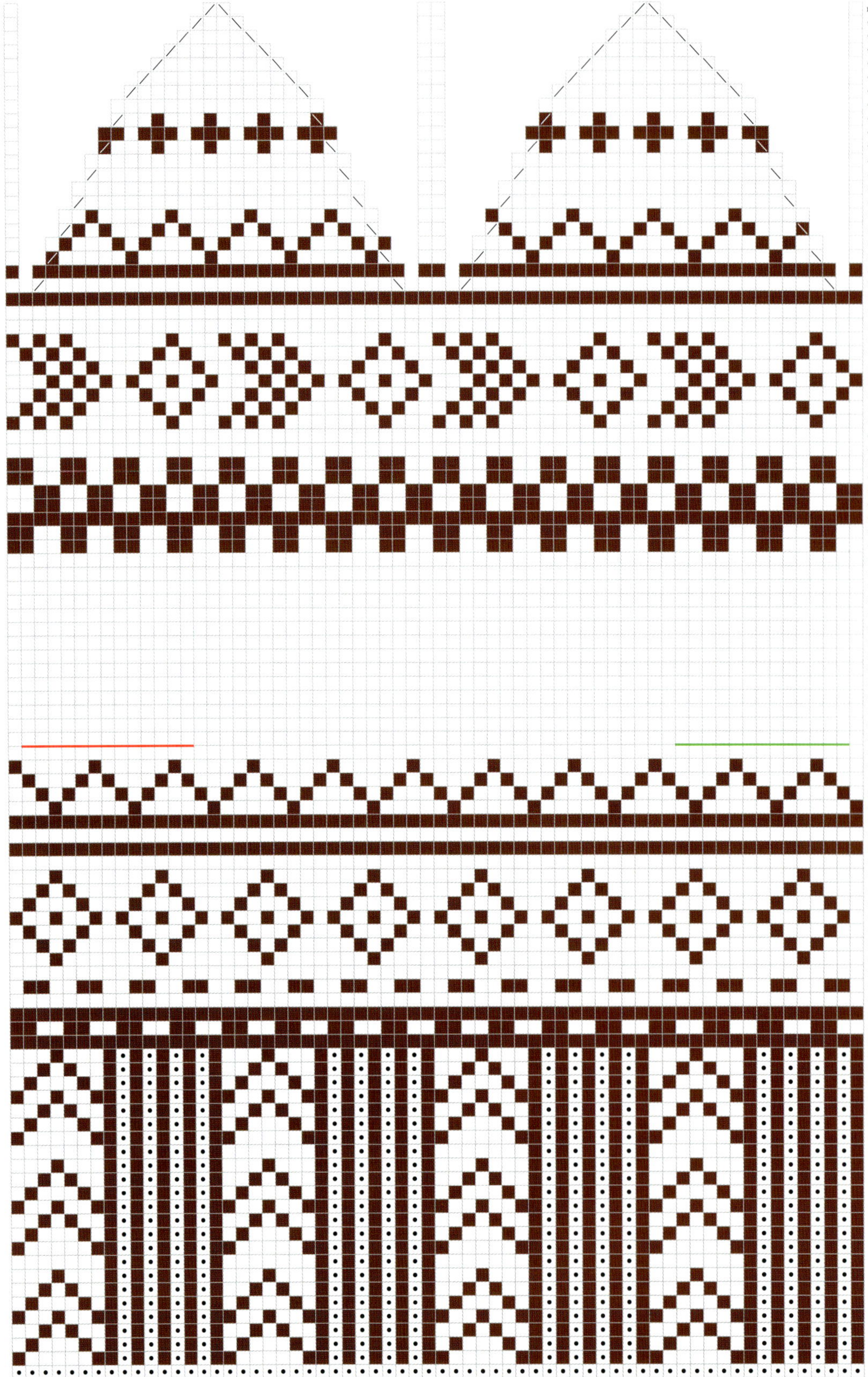

Thumb

- Knit—MC **white**
- Knit—CC **brown**
- Purl
- K2tog
- Ssk
- Sl1, k2tog, psso
- Thumb opening on left mitten
- Thumb opening on right mitten
- Pick up and knit stitches on either side of the thumb opening

FREYJA

A nice pair of minimalist knitted gloves from Halldórustofa, made by a student from the Women's School. They are knitted in two colors: brown and white. The cuff begins with a picot stitch and the edge is then turned under. The cuff is knitted in two colors, forming vertical stripes. On the backs and palms of the gloves are rows of two-color diamond patterns, while the fingers and thumbs are knitted in one color. These gloves are an easy example to try for a knitter who has already worked stranded mittens.

SIZE Women's medium

FINISHED MEASUREMENTS 11 in/27 cm long to end of middle finger (incl. 3 in/7 cm cuff) and 7 in/18 cm around palm circumference.

YARN CYCA #1 (sock/fingering/baby) *Pirkkalanka Ohut* (100% wool, 437 yd/400 m / 100 g)
Main color (MC): brownish red, 50 g.
Contrasting color (CC): off-white, 50 g.

CYCA #1 (sock/fingering/baby) *Rowan Fine Tweed* (100% wool, 98 yd/90 m / 25 g)
Main color (MC): ochre, 50 g.
Contrasting color (CC): turquoise, 50 g.

Or similar fingering weight wool.

NEEDLES Size US 0/2 mm set of 5 DPNs for the cuff. Size US 1/2.5 mm set of 5 DPNs for the hand. Adjust needle size if necessary to obtain the correct gauge.

OTHER MATERIALS Scrap yarn and tapestry needle.

GAUGE 36 sts and 40 rounds in stranded colorwork, on larger needles, after blocking = 4 in/10 cm.

If the gauge is not correct, the gloves might not fit properly.

PATTERN NOTES

- See the section beginning on page 30 for special techniques concerning yarn dominance, decreasing, increasing, and finishing.
- To finish, the picot edge of the cuff is folded and sewn under. Color dominance has to be considered when working the cuff.
- The diamond pattern is the same on the palm and the back and all the fingers and the thumbs are knitted in MC.
- Read the chart from right to left. The palm is knitted first for the right glove and the back is knitted first for the left glove.

CUFF With smaller needles and MC, cast on 62 sts. Arrange sts on the needles: 16+16+16+14 sts and join into round.

Knit 5 rounds in MC.

Round 6, picot round: [Yo, k2tog] x 31.

Rounds 7–35: *K1 with MC, k1 with CC.* Repeat from * to * to the end of the round. Read about color dominance in the section on stranded colorwork beginning on page 30.

Arrange the sts on the needles: 16+15+16+15 sts.

HAND

Change to larger needles.

Round 36 (MC), inc. round: [K15, kfb, k14, kfb] x 2 = 66 sts.

Rounds 37–59: Knit the diamond pattern from the chart.

THUMB

Round 60 (MC)**:** Work the thumb openings as follows:

RIGHT GLOVE

Knit the first 9 sts with scrap yarn (red line on the chart), slip these 9 sts back with left needle and knit in pattern to the end of the round.

LEFT GLOVE

Knit until 9 sts are left in the round. K9 sts with scrap yarn (purple line on the chart), slip these 9 sts back onto left needle and knit in pattern.

Rounds 61–77: Knit the diamond pattern from the chart.

FINGERS

All the fingers are knit with MC. The little finger is started lower than the rest and knit first, before knitting the other fingers. Sts from the back and the palm are knit as well as the sts that are cast on or picked up between each of the fingers.

LITTLE FINGER
RIGHT GLOVE

Place the next 25 sts on scrap yarn, the next 16 sts on two needles, and place the last 25 sts on scrap yarn.

LEFT GLOVE

Place the next 8 sts on a needle, next 50 sts on scrap yarn, and the last 8 sts on a needle.

Knit the 16 sts, cast on 4 sts between the little finger and the ring finger = 20 sts. Arrange the sts over 3 DPNs. The round begins in the center of the 4 cast on sts between the little and ring fingers.

Knit 22 rounds.

Round 23: [K1, ssk, k4, k2tog, k1] x 2 = 16 sts.

Round 24: Knit.

Round 25: [K1, ssk, k2, k2tog, k1] x 2 = 12 sts.

Round 26: [K1, ssk, k2tog, k1] x 2 = 8 sts.

Close the top of the finger (see the section about finishing, page 31).

Place the sts on the scrap yarn on 4 needles, starting the round by the little finger. Then pick up and knit 4 sts at the end of the round between the little finger and ring finger = 54 sts.

Knit 5 rounds.

RING FINGER

Place the 4 sts between the little and ring fingers, plus 8 sts on either side, onto DPNs and place the remaining hand sts onto scrap yarn. Cast on 4 sts between the ring finger and the middle finger = 24 sts. Arrange the sts over 3 DPNs. The round begins in the center of the 4 cast on sts between ring and middle fingers.

Knit 24 rounds.

Round 25: [K1, ssk, k6, k2tog, k1] x 2 = 20 sts.

Rounds 26 and 28: Knit.

Round 27: [K1, ssk, k4, k2tog, k1] x 2 = 16 sts.

Round 29: [K1, ssk, k2, k2tog, k1] x 2 = 12 sts.

Round 30: [K1, ssk, k2tog, k1] x 2 = 8 sts.

Close the top of the finger as before.

MIDDLE FINGER

Place the next 8 sts from scrap yarn onto a needle (from the back of the right glove and from the palm side on the left glove) and cast on 4 sts between the middle finger and the index finger. Place the last 8 sts from scrap yarn onto a needle (from the palm side of the right glove and from the back of the left glove) and pick up and knit 4 sts between the middle finger and the ring finger = 24 sts. Arrange the sts over 3 DPNs. The round begins in the center of the 4 cast on sts between middle and index fingers.

Knit 26 rounds.

Round 27: [K1, ssk, k6, k2tog, k1] x 2 = 20 sts.

Rounds 28 and 30: Knit.

Round 29: [K1, ssk, k4, k2tog, k1] x 2 = 16 sts.

Round 31: [K1, ssk, k2, k2tog, k1] x 2 = 12 sts.

Round 32: [K1, ssk, k2tog, k1] x 2 = 8 sts.

Close the top of the finger as before.

INDEX FINGER

Place the last 18 sts from scrap yarn onto 2 DPNs. Knit these 18 sts, then pick up and knit 4 sts between the index finger and the middle finger = 22 sts. Arrange the sts over 3 DPNs. The round begins in the center of the 4 picked up sts between the middle and index fingers.

Knit 24 rounds.

Round 25: [K1, ssk, k5, k2tog, k1] x 2 = 18 sts.

Round 26 and 28: Knit.

Round 27: [K1, ssk, k3, k2tog, k1] x 2 = 14 sts.

Round 29: [K1, ssk, k1, k2tog, k1] x 2 = 10 sts.

Round 30: [K1, ssk, k2] x 2 = 8 sts.

Close the top of the finger as before.

THUMB

Remove scrap yarn, place sts on 3 needles and knit around in MC, picking up 2 sts on either side of the opening and one extra stitch at the top of the opening = 22 sts.

Knit 21 rounds.

Round 22: [K4, k2tog, k3, k2tog] x 2 = 18 sts

Round 23: [K3, k2tog, k2, k2tog] x 2 = 14 sts.

Round 24: [K2, k2tog, k1, k2tog] x 2 = 10 sts.

Round 25: [K1, k2tog twice] x 2 = 6 sts.

Close the top of the thumb as before.

FINISHING

Weave in all ends. Fold the hem inward and sew it, taking care that the seam is not too tight. Wash and block both gloves, patting them gently to get the right size and to even out the stitches.

Left and right gloves

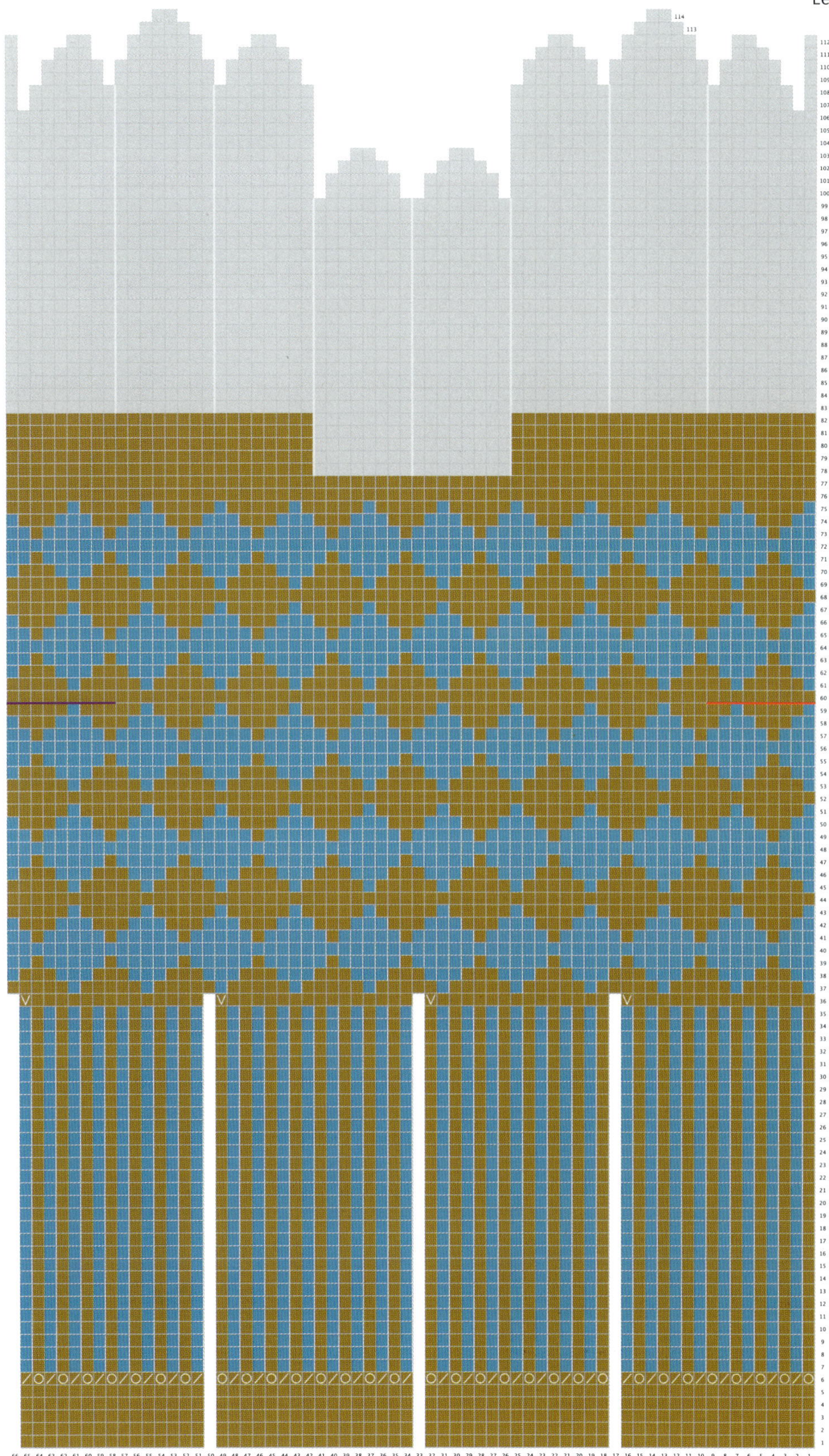

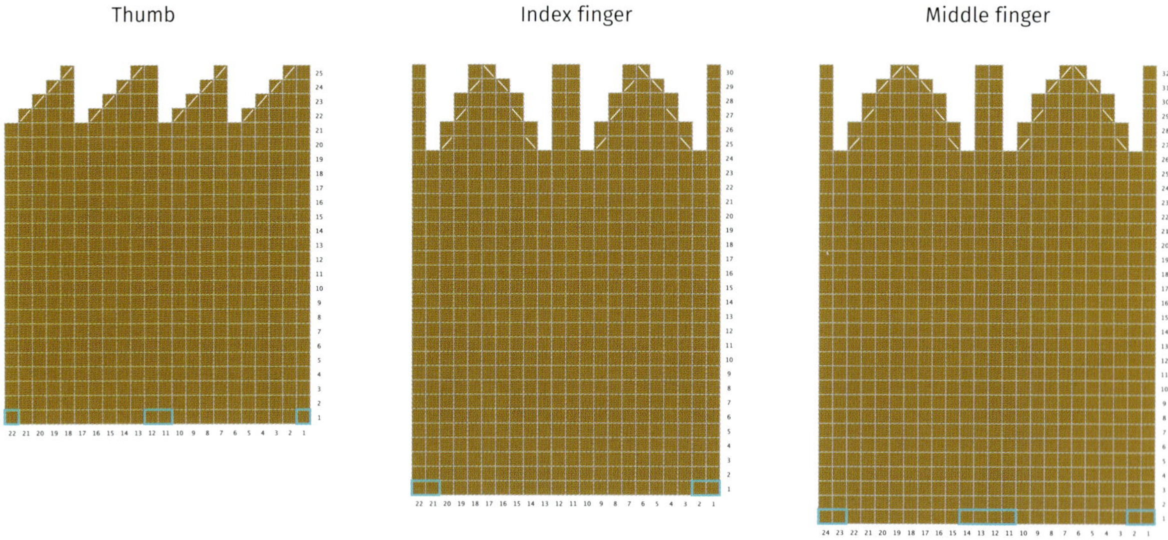
Thumb
Index finger
Middle finger

SHIMANO
Nexus

Ring finger

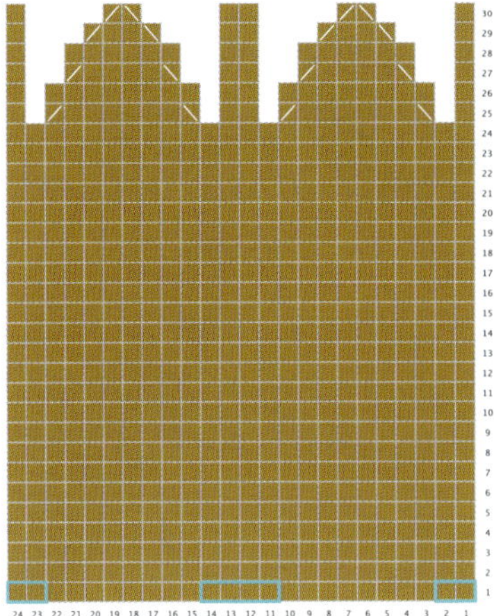

Little finger

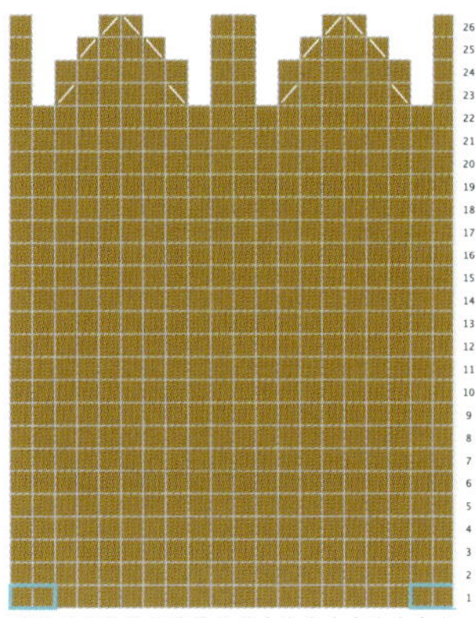

■	Knit—MC **ochre**
■	Knit—CC **turquoise**
○	YO
V	Kfb
/	K2tog
\	Ssk
	Thumb opening on left mitten
	Thumb opening on right mitten
	Outlines of fingers—knit from the finger charts
□	Pick up and knit stitches on either side of the opening and between fingers

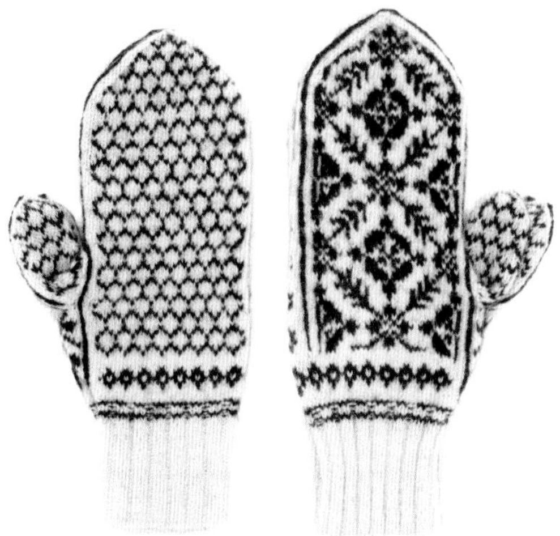

ÁSA

These beautifully patterned mittens were given to the Textile Museum in 2000. Elísabet Guðmundsdóttir (1884–1969) hand-spun the fine wool and knitted them with a white main color and a black contrast color. The cuffs are in the main color only, and the thumbs are knitted with a gusset out from the sides of the mittens. On the back of the mitten is a leaf pattern, and on the palm an all-over diamond pattern. Similar patterns have been seen in Norwegian knitting instructions, and this particular leaf pattern was published in a booklet from *Íslensk ull* (Icelandic wool) in 1944. These patterns demand concentration, as the thumb has a gusset in the back as well as the front and the charts are not necessarily easily memorized. With some patience, a beautiful result can be achieved.

SIZE Women's medium

FINISHED MEASUREMENTS 12 in/30 cm long (incl. 3 in/8 cm ribbed cuff) and 8.5 in/21 cm around palm circumference.

YARN CYCA #1 (sock/fingering/baby) *Pirkkalanka Ohut* (100% wool, 437 yd/400 m / 100 g)
Main color (MC): white, 50 g. Contrasting color (CC): black, 50 g.

CYCA #2 (sport/baby) *Mohair by Canard Kid Mohair 2-ply* (65% Mohair, 35% Merino, 193 yd/176 m / 50 g)
Main color (MC): dark grey, 50 g. Contrasting color (CC): blue green, 50 g.

Or similar fingering weight wool.

NEEDLES Size US 0/2 mm set of 5 DPNs for the cuff. Size US 1/2.5 mm set of 5 DPNs for the hand. Adjust needle size if necessary to obtain the correct gauge.

OTHER MATERIALS Scrap yarn and tapestry needle.

GAUGE 36 stitches and 38 rounds in stranded colorwork, on larger needles, after blocking = 4 in/10 cm.

If the gauge is not correct, the mittens might not fit properly.

PATTERN NOTES

- See the section beginning on page 30 for special techniques concerning yarn dominance, decreasing, increasing, and finishing.
- All stitches are knit stitches unless specifically noted otherwise.
- Read all chart rounds from right to left. The thumb is worked at the beginning of the round on the right mitten and at the end of the round on the left mitten.
- These mittens have the thumb at the side. The beginning of the thumb is marked on the chart with a red square. This marks the beginning of the thumb chart. Behind the thumb is a gusset to decrease the stitches. The beginning of the gusset is marked with a yellow square.

CUFF With MC and smaller needles, cast on 68 stitches. Arrange stitches on the needles: 16+16+16+20 stitches and join into round.

Work the cuff in k2, p2 ribbing. The first 27 rounds in MC, 1 round in CC, 2 rounds in MC and one round in CC = 31 rounds (approximately 3 in/8 cm).

Change to larger needles and work one round with MC, increasing 9 stitches in the round as follows:

RIGHT MITTEN

Round 32, inc. round: [Kfb, k7, kfb, k6] x 4, kfb, k7 = 77 stitches.

LEFT MITTEN

Round 32, inc. round: [K7, kfb, k6, kfb] x 4, k7, kfb = 77 stitches.

Increase for the thumb at the beginning of the next round for the right mitten and at the end of the round for the left mitten. The first stitch is in the red square on the chart. From there, work in pattern from the thumb chart. *At the same time*, follow the chart for the body of the mitten.

RIGHT MIITEN THUMB GUSSET

Round 33: M1L, k77 = 78 stitches.

Round 34: Knit.

Round 35: M1R, k1, M1L, k77 = 80 stitches.

Rounds 36–37: Knit.

Round 38: M1R, k3, M1L, k77 = 82 stitches.

Rounds 39–40: Knit.

Round 41: M1R, k5, M1L, k77 = 84 stitches.

Rounds 42–43: Knit.

Round 44: M1R, k7, M1L, k77 = 86 stitches.

Rounds 45–46: Knit.

Round 47: M1R, k9, M1L, k77 = 88 stitches.

Rounds 48–49: Knit.

Round 50: M1R, k11, M1L, k77 = 90 stitches.

Rounds 51–52: Knit.

Round 53: M1R, k13, M1L, k77 = 92 stitches.

Rounds 54–55: Knit.

Round 56: M1R, k15, M1L, k77 = 94 stitches.

Rounds 57–58: Knit.

LEFT MITTEN THUMB GUSSET

Round 33: K77, M1L = 78 stitches.

Round 34: Knit.

Round 35: K77, M1R, k1, M1L = 80 stitches.

Rounds 36–37: Knit.

Round 38: K77, M1R, k3, M1L = 82 stitches.

Rounds 39–40: Knit.

Round 41: K77, M1R, k5, M1L = 84 stitches.

Rounds 42–43: Knit.

Round 44: K77, M1R, k7, M1L = 86 stitches.

Rounds 45–46: Knit.

Round 47: K77, M1R, k9, M1L = 88 stitches.

Rounds 48–49: Knit.

Round 50: K77, M1R, k11, M1L = 90 stitches.

Rounds 51–52: Knit.

Round 53: K77, M1R, k13, M1L = 92 stitches.

Rounds 54–55: Knit.

Round 56: K77, M1R, k15, M1L = 94 stitches.

Rounds 57–58: Knit.

BOTH MITTENS

Round 59: Work the round in pattern, but upon reaching the thumb gusset, place 17 thumb stitches on scrap yarn. Then cast on 13 stitches which will form the thumb gusset behind the thumb (yellow stitches on the chart) = 90 stitches.

THUMB GUSSET BEHIND THE THUMB

Work the mitten from the chart and the gusset decreases *at the same time*.

RIGHT MITTEN

Rounds 60, 63, 65, 67 and 69: Knit.

Round 61: Ssk, k9, k2tog, k77 = 88 stitches.

Round 62: Ssk, k7, k2tog, k77 = 86 stitches.

Round 64: Ssk, k5, k2tog, k77 = 84 stitches.

Round 66: Ssk, k3, k2tog, k77 = 82 stitches.

Round 68: Ssk, k1, k2tog, k77 = 80 stitches.

Round 70: Sl2tog, k1, p2sso, k77 = 78 stitches.

Round 71: Slip last stitch from last round back to left needle.

Work a double decrease: Sl2tog, k1, p2sso. Knit in pattern to end of round = 76 stitches.

One stitch remains in CC, which will form a line of stitches as on the other side of the mitten.

LEFT MITTEN

Rounds 60, 63, 65, 67 and 69: Knit.

Round 61: K77, ssk, k9, k2tog = 88 stitches.

Round 62: K77, ssk, k7, k2tog = 86 stitches.

Round 64: K77, ssk, k5, k2tog = 84 stitches.

Round 66: K77, ssk, k3, k2tog = 82 stitches.

Round 68: K77, ssk, k1, k2tog = 80 stitches.

Round 70: K77, sl2tog, k1, p2sso = 78 stitches.

Round 71: Knit in pattern until 2 stitches remain in round. Work a double decrease: Sl2tog, k1, p2sso (2 last stitches in round and first stitch in next round) = 76 stitches. Slip last stitch just worked back to left needle.

One stitch remains in CC, which will form a line of stitches as on the other side of the mitten.

Continue knitting the mitten from the chart until round 98 is reached.

DECREASE

Decreases are worked 4 times on every round.

RIGHT MITTEN

Round 98: [Ssk, k33, k2tog, k1] x 2 = 72 stitches.

Round 99: [Ssk, k31, k2tog, k1] x 2 = 68 stitches.

Round 100: [Ssk, k29, k2tog, k1] x 2 = 64 stitches.

Round 101: [Ssk, k27, k2tog, k1] x 2 = 60 stitches.

Round 102: [Ssk, k25, k2tog, k1] x 2 = 56 stitches.

Round 103: [Ssk, k23, k2tog, k1] x 2 = 52 stitches.

Round 104: [Ssk, k21, k2tog, k1] x 2 = 48 stitches.

Round 105: [Ssk, k19, k2tog, k1] x 2 = 44 stitches.

Round 106: [Ssk, k17, k2tog, k1] x 2 = 40 stitches.

Round 107: [Ssk, k15, k2tog, k1] x 2 = 36 stitches.

Round 108: [Ssk, k13, k2tog, k1] x 2 = 32 stitches.

Round 109: [Ssk, k11, k2tog, k1] x 2 = 28 stitches.

Round 110: [Ssk, k9, k2tog, k1] x 2 = 24 stitches.

Round 111: [Ssk, k7, k2tog, k1] x 2 = 20 stitches.

Round 112: [Ssk, k5, k2tog, k1] x 2 = 16 stitches.

Round 113: [Ssk, k3, k2tog, k1] x 2 = 12 stitches.

Round 114: [Ssk, k1, k2tog, k1] x 2 = 8 stitches.

LEFT MITTEN

The decreases are the same as for the left mitten except the round starts with k1.

Round 98: [K1, ssk, k33, k2tog] x 2 = 72 stitches. Continue in the same manner and after round 114 there should be 8 stitches left.

FINISHING THE TOP OF THE MITTEN

Close the top of the mitten (see the section about finishing, page 31).

THUMB Divide the 17 stitches from scrap yarn over 2 dpns. Pick up and knit 13 stitches behind the thumb (green line on the chart) with the 3rd dpn = 30 thumb stitches. Work in pattern from the chart and start decreasing on round 20.

Round 20: [K2, ssk, k9, k2tog] x 2 = 26 stitches.

Round 21: [K2, ssk, k7, k2tog] x 2 = 22 stitches.

Round 22: [K2, ssk, k5, k2tog] x 2 = 18 stitches.

Round 23: [K2, ssk, k3, k2tog] x 2 = 14 stitches.

Round 24: [K2, ssk, k1, k2tog] x 2 = 10 stitches.

Round 25: K2, ssk, k3, ssk, k1 = 8 stitches.

Close the top of the thumb in the same way as the top of the mitten.

FINISHING Weave in all ends. Wash and block both mittens, patting them gently to get the right size and to even out the stitches.

Left mitten

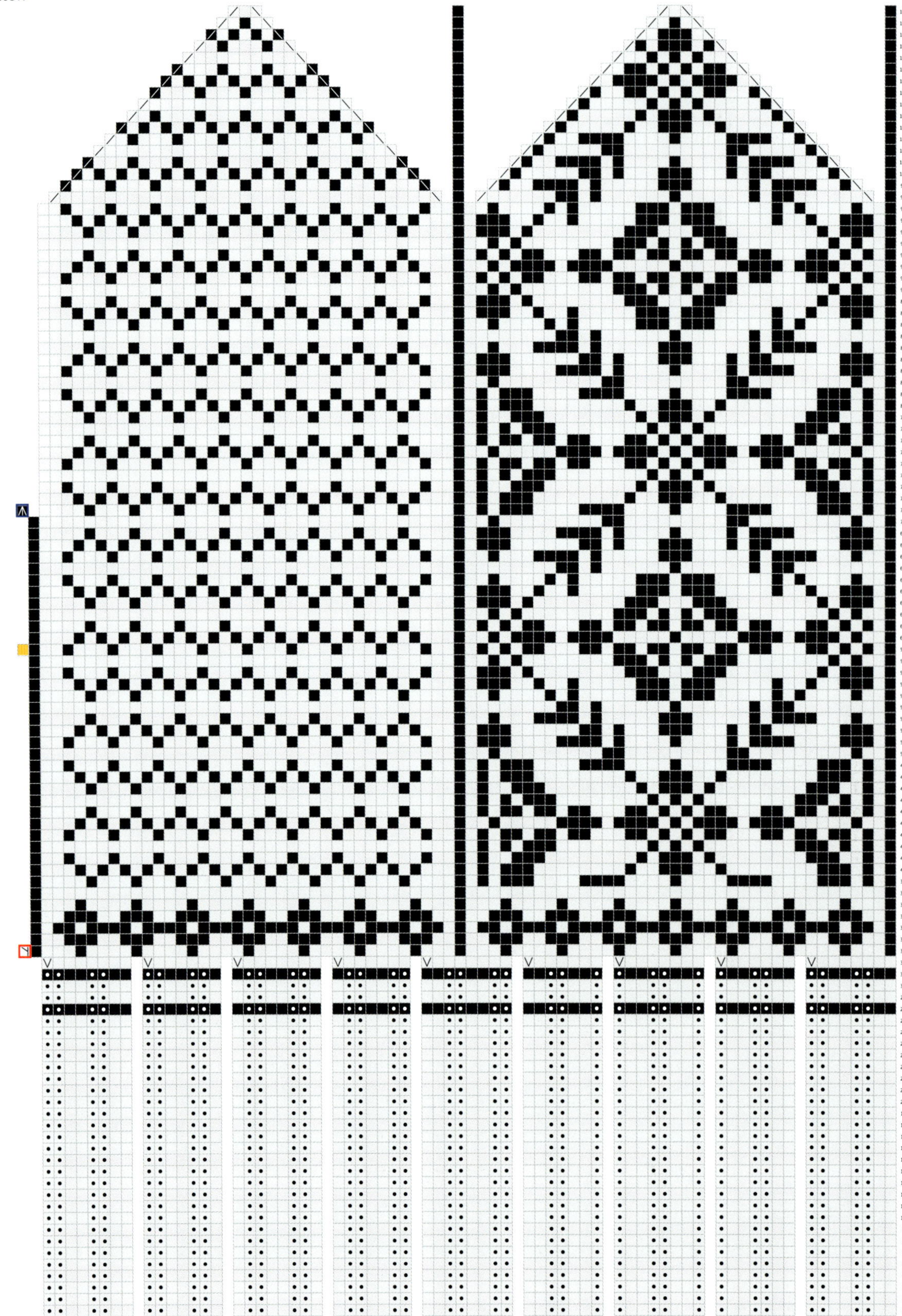

Right mitten

Thumb and thumb gusset

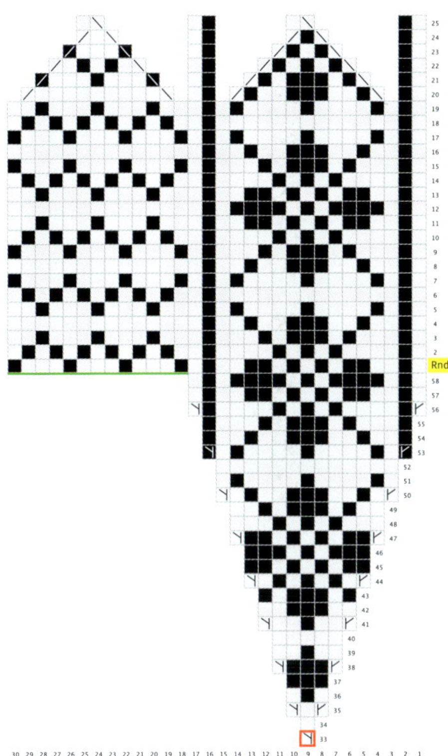

Gusset behind the thumb

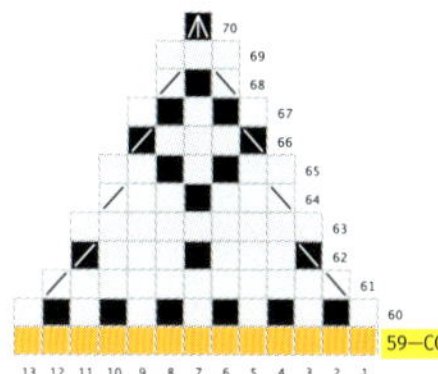

- Knit—MC **white**
- Knit—CC **black**
- Purl
- K2tog
- Ssk
- Pick up and knit stitches behind the thumb
- S2tog, k1, p2sso
- Kfb
- M1L
- M1R
- Pick up and knit stitches behind the thumb
- Start thumb gusset
- End gusset behind the thumb

LÓA

An interesting example of mittens in one of the traditional West Fjords pattern styles. They have colorful patterned bands at the top and bottom. These are called *laufviðarvettlingar*, or "leaf mittens," and were made during one of Halldóra Bjarnadóttir's competitions. The patterns may be classic, but the choice of color is unusual. The main color is off-white and the contrast colors are black, red, pink, and purple. They are cast on with purple. Typical of mittens from the West Fjords, these have very short ribbed cuffs followed by stranded patterns. Be careful to keep the tension even whether knitting with one color or with two.

SIZE Women's medium

FINISHED MEASUREMENTS 10.5 in/26 cm long and 7 in/18 cm around palm circumference.

YARN CYCA #1 (sock/fingering/baby) *Pirkkalanka Ohut* (100% wool, 437 yd/400 m / 100 g) Main color (MC): light beige, 50 g. Contrasting colors (CC): purple, dark pink, light pink, black, 25 g of each.

CYCA #1 (sock/fingering/baby) *Rowan Fine Tweed* (100% wool, 98 yd/90 m / 25 g) Main color (MC): curry yellow, 50 g. Contrasting colors (CC): blue, dark pink, ochre, black, 25 g of each.

Or similar fingering weight wool.

NEEDLES Size US 0/2 mm set of 5 DPNs for the cuff. Size US 1/2.5 mm set of 5 DPNs for the hand. Adjust needle size if necessary to obtain the correct gauge.

OTHER MATERIALS Scrap yarn and tapestry needle.

GAUGE 34 stitches and 44 rounds in stranded colorwork, on larger needles, after blocking = 4 in/10 cm.

If the gauge is not correct, the mittens might not fit properly.

PATTERN NOTES

- See the section beginning on page 30 for special techniques concerning yarn dominance, decreasing, increasing, and finishing.
- All stitches are knit stitches unless specifically noted otherwise.
- Both mittens are knitted from the same chart.
- Read all chart rounds from right to left.
- The thumb is worked at the beginning of the round on the right mitten and at the end of the round on the left mitten.
- Some knitters knit tighter when knitting stranded colorwork. So it may be necessary to change needle sizes when changing from single-color to stranded knitting in order to maintain gauge.

CUFF

With smaller needles and blue yarn, cast on 60 stitches. Arrange stitches on the needles: 15+15+15+15 stitches and join into round.

Change to MC and work 13 rounds in k2, p1 rib.

Knit 1 round with MC and then work following the chart for rounds 15–23.

HAND

Change to larger needles and ochre yarn, and work one increase round as follows:

Round 24, inc. round: [K14, kfb] x 4 = 64 stitches. Now there are 16 stitches on each needle.

Follow the chart for the stranded knitting until round 37.

Round 37, inc. round: [K31, kfb] x 2 = 66 stitches.

Now there are 16+17+16+17 stitches on the needles.

Follow the chart for the stranded knitting until round 50.

Round 50: Work the thumb openings as follows:

RIGHT MITTEN

K1, k11 with scrap yarn (green line on the chart), slip these 11 stitches back onto the left needle and knit in pattern to the end of the round.

LEFT MITTEN

Knit until 12 stitches are left in the round. K11 stitches with scrap yarn (red line on the chart), slip these 11 stitches back onto left needle and knit in pattern to the end of the round.

BOTH MITTENS

Knit the hand with MC until the beginning of round 79 on the chart. Knit in stranded colorwork until beginning the decreases on round 86.

START DECREASE ROUNDS

Work in pattern from the chart while working decreases.

Round 86: [Ssk, k31] x 2 = 64 stitches.

Rounds 87–89: Knit.

Next, decrease 4 stitches across the round, every alternate round 5 times and then every round 9 times.

Round 90: [Ssk, k28, k2tog] x 2 = 60 stitches.

Rounds 91, 93, 95, 97, and 99: Knit.

Round 92: [Ssk, k26, k2tog] x 2 = 56 stitches.

Round 94: [Ssk, k24, k2tog] x 2 = 52 stitches.

Round 96: [Ssk, k22, k2tog] x 2 = 48 stitches.

Round 98: [Ssk, k20, k2tog] x 2 = 44 stitches.

Round 100: [Ssk, k18, k2tog] x 2 = 40 stitches.

Round 101: [Ssk, k16, k2tog] x 2 = 36 stitches.

Round 102: [Ssk, k14, k2tog] x 2 = 32 stitches.

Round 103: [Ssk, k12, k2tog] x 2 = 28 stitches.

Round 104: [Ssk, k10, k2tog] x 2 = 24 stitches.

Round 105: [Ssk, k8, k2tog] x 2 = 20 stitches.

Round 106: [Ssk, k6, k2tog] x 2 = 16 stitches.

Round 107: [Ssk, k4, k2tog] x 2 = 12 stitches.

Round 108: [Ssk, k2, k2tog] x 2 = 8 stitches.

Close the top of the mitten (see the section about finishing, page 31).

THUMB

Remove scrap yarn, place stitches on 3 needles and knit around in pattern, picking up 2 stitches on either side of the opening and one extra stitch at the top of the opening = 26 stitches.

Work in pattern from the chart and start decreasing on round 20.

Round 20: [Ssk, k5, ssk, k4] x 2 = 22 stitches.

Round 21: Knit.

Round 22: [Ssk, k4, ssk, k3] x 2 = 18 stitches.

Round 23: Knit.

Round 24: [Ssk, k3, ssk, k2] x 2 = 14 stitches.

Round 25: [Ssk, k5] x 2 = 12 stitches.

Round 26: [Ssk, k1] x 4 = 8 stitches.

Round 27: [Ssk] x 4 = 4 stitches.

Close the top of the thumb in the same way as the top of the mitten.

FINISHING

Weave in all ends. Wash and block both mittens, patting them gently to get the right size and to even out the stitches.

Left and right mittens

CO with CC

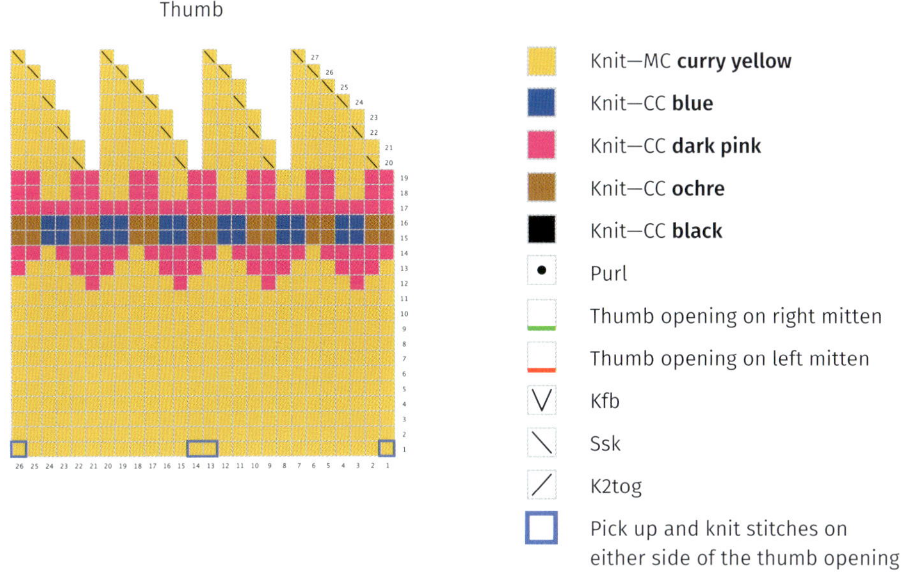
Thumb
Knit—MC **curry yellow**
Knit—CC **blue**
Knit—CC **dark pink**
Knit—CC **ochre**
Knit—CC **black**
Purl
Thumb opening on right mitten
Thumb opening on left mitten
Kfb
Ssk
K2tog
Pick up and knit stitches on either side of the thumb opening

SVALA

These mittens of unknown origin also come from Halldórustofa. The original mittens are knitted in 3-ply natural colors: brown, white, and grey. The body of each mitten is a pattern of squares and diamonds which is repeated on the thumb. These mittens have a ribbed cuff and an afterthought thumb. This is a fairly simple pattern and perfect for practicing stranded knitting.

SIZE Women's medium

FINISHED MEASUREMENTS 11 in/27.5 cm long (incl. 3 in/7.5 cm ribbed cuff) and 7 in/18 cm around palm circumference.

YARN CYCA #1 (sock/fingering/baby) *Pirkkalanka Ohut* (100% wool, 437 yd/400 m / 100 g)
Main color (MC): light brown, 50 g.
Contrasting color (CC): off-white and grey, 50 g of each.

CYCA #1 (sock/fingering/baby) *Rowan Fine Tweed* (100% wool, 98 yd/90 m / 25 g)
Main color (MC): light grey, 50 g.
Contrasting color (CC): dark grey, 50 g, and light grey, 25 g.

Or similar fingering weight wool.

NEEDLES Size US 0/2 mm set of 5 DPNs for the cuff. Size US 1/2.5 mm set of 5 DPNs for the hand. Adjust needle size if necessary to obtain the correct gauge.

OTHER MATERIALS Scrap yarn and tapestry needle.

GAUGE 38 stitches and 38 rounds in stranded colorwork, on larger needles, after blocking = 4 in/10 cm.

If the gauge is not correct, the mittens might not fit properly.

PATTERN NOTES

- See the section beginning on page 30 for special techniques concerning yarn dominance, decreasing, increasing, and finishing.
- All stitches are knit stitches unless specifically noted otherwise.
- Both mittens are knitted from the same chart.
- Read all chart rounds from right to left.
- The thumb is worked at the beginning of the round on the right mitten and at the end of the round on the left mitten.

CUFF

With smaller needles and MC, cast on 68 stitches. Arrange stitches on the needles: 20+16+16+16 stitches and join into round. Work 30 rounds (3 in/7.5 cm) of ribbing: k2, p2.

HAND

Rearrange stitches so there are 17 stitches on each of the four needles.

Round 31, inc. round: [K17, M1L] x 4 = 72 stitches.

Change to larger needles. Work in pattern from the chart to round 54.

Round 54: Work in pattern from the chart while working thumb openings:

RIGHT MITTEN

K1, k13 stitches with scrap yarn (green line on the chart), slip these 13 stitches back onto left needle and knit in pattern to the end of the round.

LEFT MITTEN

Knit until 14 stitches are left in the round. K13 stitches with scrap yarn (red line on the chart). Slip these 13 stitches back onto left needle and knit in pattern to the end of the round.

BOTH MITTENS

Work in pattern from the chart to round 94.

START DECREASE ROUNDS

Start decrease rounds: Work in pattern from the chart while working decreases.

Decrease 4 stitches on the indicated rounds as follows:

Round 94: [Ssk, k31, k2tog, k1] x 2 = 68 stitches.

Rounds 95, 97, 99, and 101: Knit.

Round 96: [Ssk, k29, k2tog, k1] x 2 = 64 stitches.

Round 98: [Ssk, k27, k2tog, k1] x 2 = 60 stitches.

Round 100: [Ssk, k25, k2tog, k1] x 2 = 56 stitches.

Round 102: [Ssk, k23, k2tog, k1] x 2 = 52 stitches.

Round 103: [Ssk, k21, k2tog, k1] x 2 = 48 stitches.

Round 104: [Ssk, k19, k2tog, k1] x 2 = 44 stitches.

Round 105: [Ssk, k17, k2tog, k1] x 2 = 40 stitches.

Round 106: [Ssk, k15, k2tog, k1] x 2 = 36 stitches.

Round 107: [Ssk, k13, k2tog, k1] x 2 = 32 stitches.

Round 108: [Ssk, k11, k2tog, k1] x 2 = 28 stitches.

Round 109: [Ssk, k9, k2tog, k1] x 2 = 24 stitches.

Round 110: [Ssk, k7, k2tog, k1] x 2 = 20 stitches.

Round 111: [Ssk, k5, k2tog, k1] x 2 = 16 stitches.

Round 112: [Ssk, k3, k2tog, k1] x 2 = 12 stitches.

Round 113: [Ssk, k1, k2tog, k1] x 2 = 8 stitches.

Close the top of the mitten (see the section about finishing, page 31).

THUMB

Remove scrap yarn, place stitches on 3 needles and knit around in pattern, picking up 2 stitches on either side of the opening and one extra stitch at the top of the opening = 30 stitches. Work in pattern from the chart and start decreasing on round 24.

Round 24: [K5, k2tog, k6, k2tog] x 2 = 26 stitches.

Round 25: [K4, k2tog, k5, k2tog] x 2 = 22 stitches.

Round 26: [K3, k2tog, k4, k2tog] x 2 = 18 stitches.

Round 27: [K2, k2tog, k3, k2tog] x 2 = 14 stitches.

Round 28: [K1, k2tog, k2, k2tog] x 2 = 10 stitches.

Round 29: [K2tog, k1, k2tog] x 2 = 6 stitches.

Close the top of the thumb in the same way as the top of the mitten.

FINISHING

Weave in all ends. Wash and block both mittens, patting them gently to get the right size and to even out the stitches.

Left and right mittens

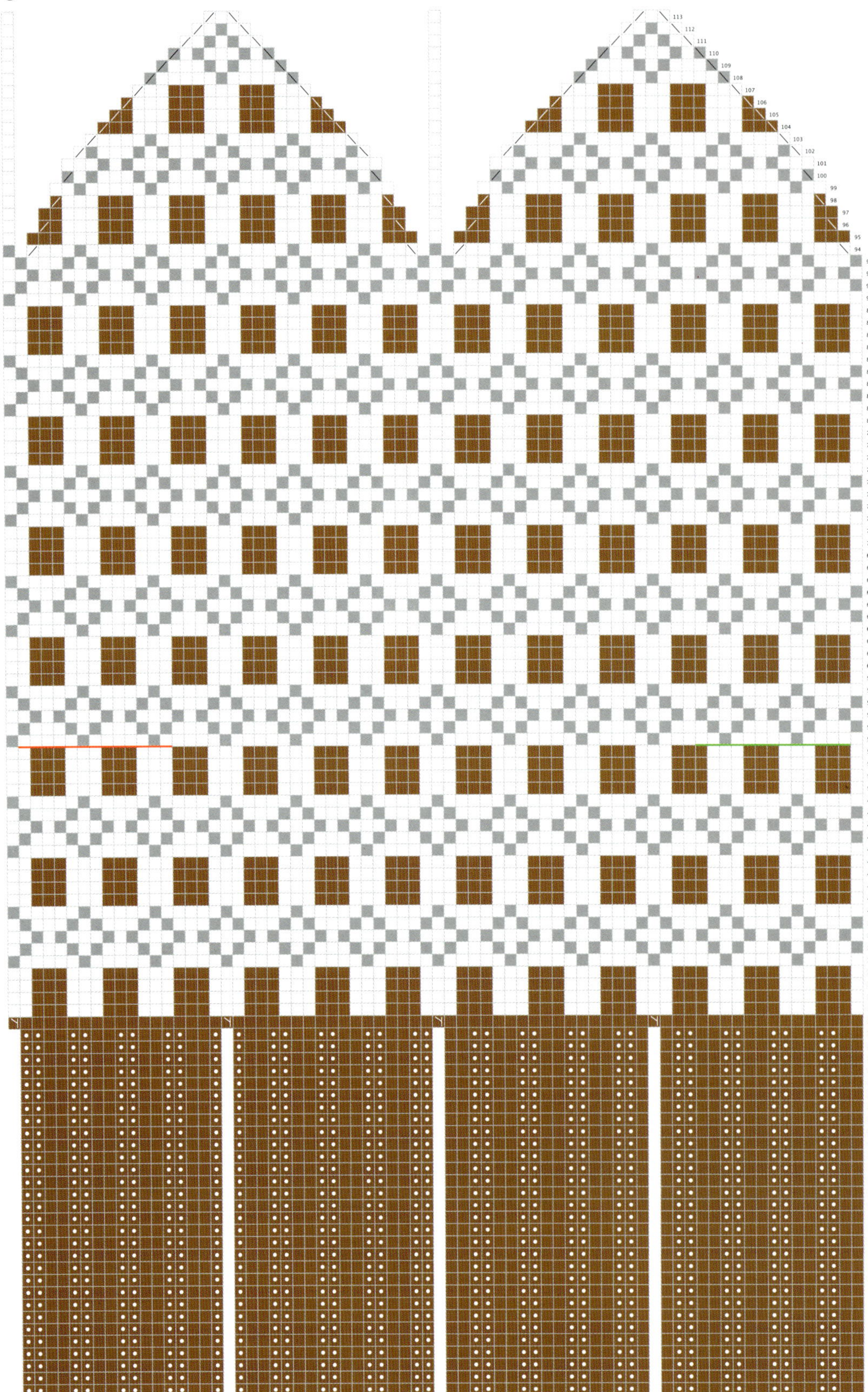

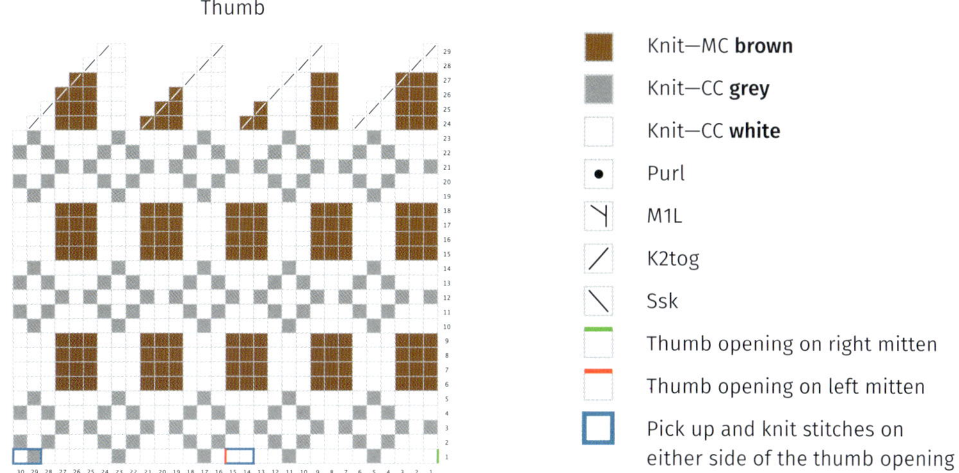
Thumb
Knit—MC **brown**
Knit—CC **grey**
Knit—CC **white**
Purl
M1L
K2tog
Ssk
Thumb opening on right mitten
Thumb opening on left mitten
Pick up and knit stitches on either side of the thumb opening

HALLA

These multi-patterned mittens are from the Textile Museum and were knit by Jóhanna Finnsdóttir (1866–1960). Jóhanna was born in Arneshreppur on Strandir and lived there until she later moved to Reykjavík. Her descendants donated these mittens to the collection in 2014. These traditional, thoroughly patterned mittens are knitted with an afterthought thumb. They are knitted with a very fine, hand-spun 2-ply wool in six natural wool colors. A similar pair was shown in a book published in 1981 by the Icelandic Handcrafts Association. The origin of the pattern is unknown. These mittens are an exciting project for anyone feeling comfortable with complex two-color stranded knitting.

SIZE	Women's medium
FINISHED MEASUREMENTS	11.5 in/29 cm long (incl. 3.5 in/9 cm cuff) and 7 in/18 cm palm circumference.
YARN	CYCA #1 (sock/fingering/baby) *Pirkkalanka Ohut* (100% wool, 437 yd/400 m / 100 g) Main color (MC): reddish, light brown, 50 g. Contrasting colors (CC): white, light grey, reddish brown, black, dark reddish brown, 25 g of each. CYCA #2 (sport/baby) *Mohair by Canard Kid Mohair 2-ply* (65% Mohair, 35% Merino, 193 yd/176 m / 50 g) Main color (MC): turquoise, 50 g. Contrasting colors (CC): grey, white, dark grey, yellow, 25 g of each. Or similar fingering weight wool.
NEEDLES	Size US 0/2 mm set of 5 DPNs for the cuff. Size US 1/2.5 mm set of 5 DPNs for the hand. Adjust needle size if necessary to obtain the correct gauge.
OTHER MATERIALS	Scrap yarn and tapestry needle.
GAUGE	36 stitches and 38 rounds in stranded colorwork, on larger needles, after blocking = 4 in/10 cm. If the gauge is not correct, the mittens might not fit properly.
PATTERN NOTES	• See the section beginning on page 30 for special techniques concerning yarn dominance, decreasing, increasing, and finishing. • All stitches are knit stitches unless specifically noted otherwise. • Both mittens are knitted from the same chart. • Read all chart rounds from right to left. • The thumb is worked at the beginning of the round on the right mitten and at the end of the round on the left mitten.

CUFF

With smaller needles and MC, cast on 60 stitches. Arrange evenly on the needles (15 stitches on each needle) and join into round.

Work cuff with wave pattern as follows: 8 rounds with reddish brown, 5 rounds with dark brown, 4 rounds with grey, and 2 rounds with white.

Round 1: Knit.

Round 2: K2, [sl2tog, k1, p2sso, k4, yo, k1, yo, k4] x 4, sl2tog, k1, p2sso, k4, yo, k1, yo, k2.

Round 3: Knit.

Rounds 4–19: Repeat rounds 2 and 3.

HAND

Round 20, inc. round: [K15, M1L] x 4 = 64 stitches.

Change to larger needles and work in pattern from the chart to round 55.

Round 55: Work in pattern from the chart while working thumb openings:

RIGHT MITTEN

K12 stitches with scrap yarn (green line on the chart), slip these 12 stitches back onto left needle and knit in pattern to the end of the round.

LEFT MITTEN

Knit until 12 stitches are left in the round. K12 stitches with scrap yarn (red line on the chart), slip these 12 stitches back onto left needle and knit in pattern to the end of the round.

BOTH MITTENS

Work in pattern from the chart to round 96.

START DECREASE ROUNDS

Work in pattern from the chart while working decreases. Decrease 4 stitches on every round as follows:

Round 96: [K14, k2tog] x 4 = 60 stitches.

Round 97: [K13, k2tog] x 4 = 56 stitches.

Round 98: [K12, k2tog] x 4 = 52 stitches.

Round 99: [K11, k2tog] x 4 = 48 stitches.

Round 100: [K10, k2tog] x 4 = 44 stitches.

Round 101: [K9, k2tog] x 4 = 40 stitches.

Round 102: [K8, k2tog] x 4 = 36 stitches.

Round 103: [K7, k2tog] x 4 = 32 stitches.

Round 104: [K6, k2tog] x 4 = 28 stitches.

Round 105: [K5, k2tog] x 4 = 24 stitches.

Round 106: [K4, k2tog] x 4 = 20 stitches.

Round 107: [K3, k2tog] x 4 = 16 stitches.

Round 108: [K2, k2tog] x 4 = 12 stitches.

Round 109: [K1, k2tog] x 4 = 8 stitches.

Round 110: [K2tog] x 4 = 4 stitches.

THUMB

Close the top of the mitten (see the section about finishing, page 31).

Remove scrap yarn, place stitches on 3 needles and knit around in pattern, picking up 2 stitches on either side of the opening and one extra stitch at the top of the opening = 28 stitches. Work in pattern from the chart and start decreasing on round 22.

Round 22: [Ssk, k9, k2tog, k1] x 2 = 24 stitches.

Round 23: [Ssk, k7, k2tog, k1] x 2 = 20 stitches.

Round 24: [Ssk, k5, k2tog, k1] x 2 = 16 stitches.

Round 25: [Ssk, k3, k2tog, k1] x 2 = 12 stitches.

Round 26: [Ssk, k1, k2tog, k1] x 2 = 8 stitches.

Round 27: [Sl1, k2tog, psso, k1] x 2 = 4 stitches.

Close the top of the thumb in the same way as the top of the mitten.

FINISHING

Weave in all ends. Wash and block both mittens, patting them gently to get the right size and to even out the stitches.

Left and right mittens

Thumb

(white square)	Knit—MC **white**
(light reddish brown square)	Knit—CC **light reddish brown**
(light grey square)	Knit—CC **light grey**
(reddish brown square)	Knit—CC **reddish brown**
(black square)	Knit—CC **black**
(dark reddish brown square)	Knit—CC **dark reddish brown**
(M1L symbol)	M1L
/	K2tog
\	Ssk
(Sl2tog symbol)	Sl2tog, k1, p2sso
∧	Sl1, k2tog, psso
○	YO
(red line)	Thumb opening on left mitten
(green line)	Thumb opening on right mitten
(blue box)	Pick up and knit stitches on either side of the thumb opening

GRÍMA

These mittens are unusual in that they are knitted sideways. According to information from the Textile Museum, they were knitted by an unknown student from the Iceland College of Education. The main color is brown and the stripes are white. They are knitted in garter stitch and sewn together on the thumb side; the thumb is knitted separately and sewn onto the mitten. Stitches are picked up and knit for the cuff, which is worked in the round with white stripes. These mittens are simple to knit, but a bit of time has to be spent finishing them. An enjoyable project for the knitter who wants to try a different kind of mitten.

SIZE	Women's medium
FINISHED MEASUREMENTS	10.5 in/26 cm long (incl. 3 in/7 cm ribbed cuff) and 7 in/18 cm around palm circumference.
YARN	CYCA #1 (sock/fingering/baby) *Pirkkalanka Ohut* (100% wool, 437 yd/400 m / 100 g) Main color (MC): light brown, 50 g. Contrasting color (CC): off white, 50 g. CYCA #1 (sock/fingering/baby) *Rowan Fine Tweed* (100% wool, 98 yd/90 m / 25 g) Main color (MC): dark brown, 50 g. Contrasting color (CC): blue, 50 g. Or similar fingering weight wool.
NEEDLES	Size US 0/2 mm set of 5 DPNs, plus optional needles in the same size for working flat if preferred. Adjust needle size if necessary to obtain the correct gauge.
OTHER MATERIALS	Tapestry needle.
GAUGE	28 stitches and 56 rows in garter stitch, after blocking, unstretched = 4 in/10 cm. If the gauge is not correct, the mittens might not fit properly.

PATTERN NOTES

- See the section beginning on page 30 for special techniques concerning yarn dominance, decreasing, increasing, and finishing.
- These mittens are knitted flat and sideways, in garter stitch.
- Start at the hand on the same side as the thumb and knit across the back and then the palm, decreasing for the top of the mitten *at the same time*.
- The thumb is knitted separately.
- The sides and top of the mitten on the thumb side are sewn together and the thumb sewn to the body *at the same time*.
- Finally, stitches are picked up at the bottom of the body and a cuff is knitted.
- Both mittens are worked the same way.

STRIPES

The mittens are worked in two colors and striped lengthwise. Each stripe is two garter stitch rows. Colors are always changed on the same side, which makes it unnecessary to break the yarn between rows.

This pattern and chart show the stripes beginning with MC, but knitters can also choose which color to begin with. The cuff is worked down from the body and begins with MC.

BOTH MITTENS

HAND

With MC and needles for working flat, cast on 54 stitches.

Row 1 (WS) and all WS rows: Knit. Change color.

Row 2 (RS): Ssk, knit to end = 53 stitches.

Decrease at the beginning of right side rows a total of 12 times = 42 stitches.

Row 26 (RS): Kfb, knit to end = 43 stitches.

Increase at the beginning of right side rows a total of 12 times = 54 stitches.

Row 50 (RS): Ssk, knit to end = 53 stitches.

Decrease at the beginning of right side rows a total of 12 times = 42 stitches.

Row 74 (RS): Kfb, knit to end = 43 stitches.

Increase at the beginning of right side rows a total of 12 times = 54 stitches.

Row 98 (RS): Knit.

Row 99 (WS): Knit.

Bind off.

THUMB

The thumb is striped and worked in the same way as the body of the mitten except the decreases and increases are at the beginning and end of the right side rows.

With MC and needles for working flat (or DPNs), cast on 16 stitches.

Row 1 (WS) and all WS rows: Knit. Change color.

Row 2 (RS): Ssk, k13, kfb = 16 stitches.

Rows 4, 6, 8, 10 and 12: Repeat row 2.

Row 14 (RS): Kfb, k14, kfb = 18 stitches.

Row 16: Kfb, k16, kfb = 20 stitches.

Row 18: Kfb, k18, kfb = 22 stitches.

Row 20: Kfb, k20, kfb = 24 stitches.

Row 22: Kfb, k22, kfb = 26 stitches.

Row 24: Kfb, k24, kfb = 28 stitches.

Row 26: Ssk, k24, k2tog = 26 stitches.

Row 28: Ssk, k22, k2tog = 24 stitches.

Row 30: Ssk, k20, k2tog = 22 stitches.

Row 32: Ssk, k18, k2tog = 20 stitches.

Row 34: Ssk, k16, k2tog = 18 stitches.

Row 36: Ssk, k14, k2tog = 16 stitches.

Row 38 (RS): Kfb, k13, k2tog = 16 stitches.

Rows 40, 42, 44 and 46: Repeat row 38.

Row 47 (WS)**:** Knit.

Bind off.

HAND AND THUMB ASSEMBLY

Sew the sides of the hand together (cast-on and bound-off edges), leaving a 3 in/7 cm opening at the bottom for the thumb and thumb gusset.

Sew the sides of the thumb together (cast-on and bound-off edges).

Sew the thumb gusset to both sides of the opening in the hand side seam.

Sew the remaining gap in the hand side seam after the thumb gusset has been fixed in place.

Lay the body together so that it forms a V at the top. Sew the opening together by threading the needle through each garter stitch bump on the edges at either side so the stitching is fine and even.

Sew the top of the thumb in the same way. Weave in ends.

Place the body flat so the top stitching is in the middle of the mitten. The seam will become even after the mittens have been blocked.

CUFF

Using DPNs, pick up and knit 50 stitches along the bottom edge of the mitten—1 stitch in every garter ridge. Arrange stitches on the needles: 12+12+12+14 stitches.

Work the cuff in k1, p1 rib.

Work 4 rounds in MC, 2 rounds in CC, 3 rounds in MC, 2 rounds in CC, 2 rounds in MC, 1 round in CC, 2 rounds in MC, 2 rounds in CC, 3 rounds in MC, 2 rounds in CC, 5 rounds in MC.

Bind off loosely.

FINISHING

Weave in all remaining ends. Wash and block both mittens, patting them gently to get the right size and to even out the stitches.

Left and right mittens

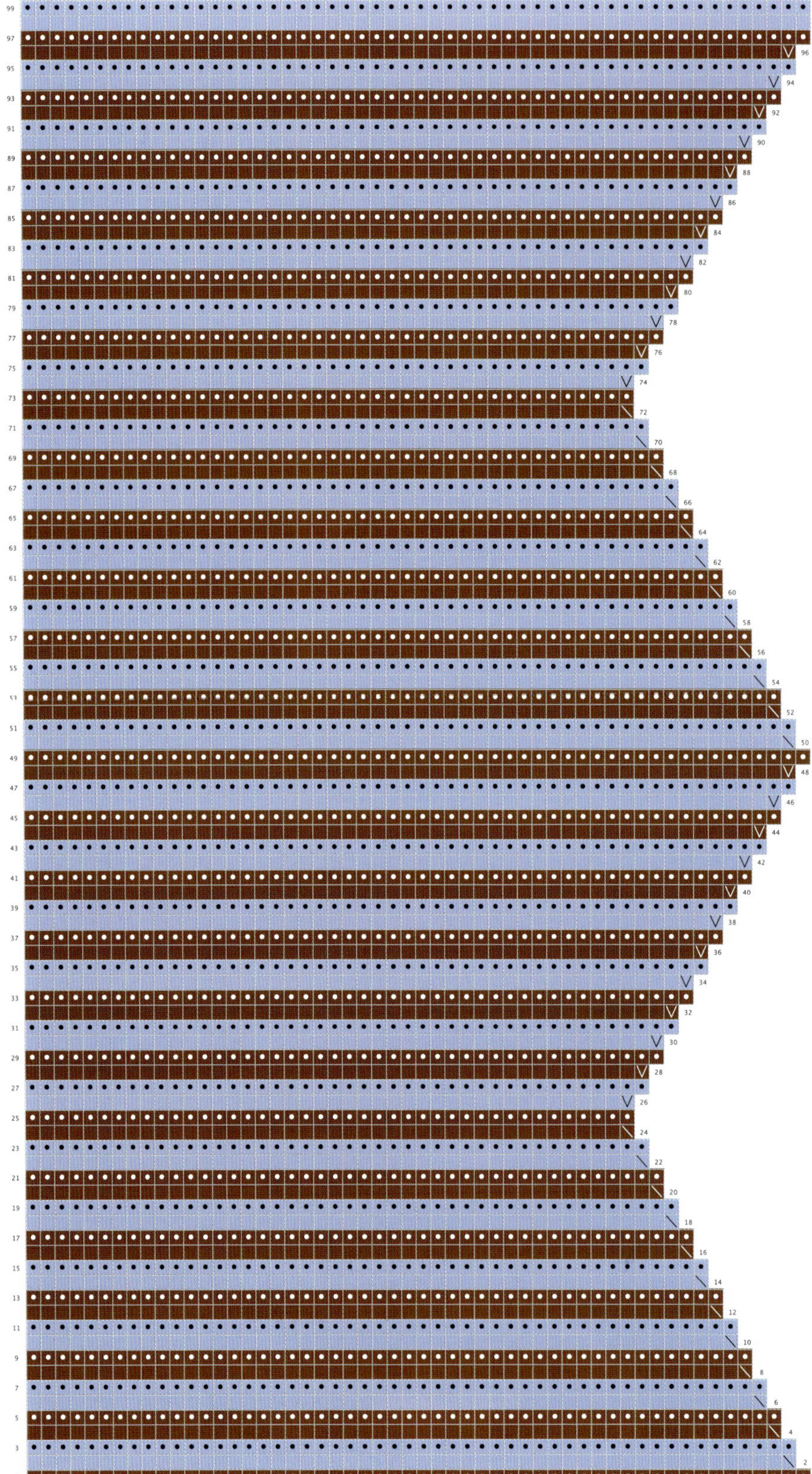

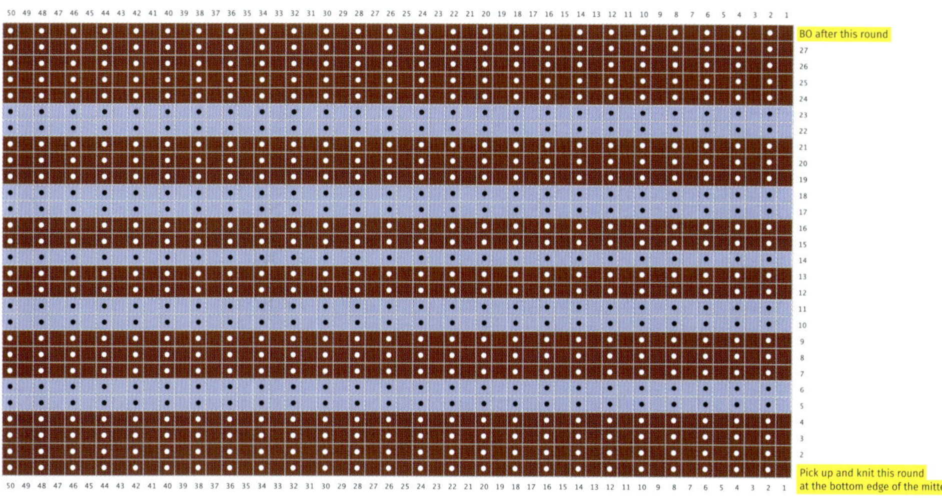

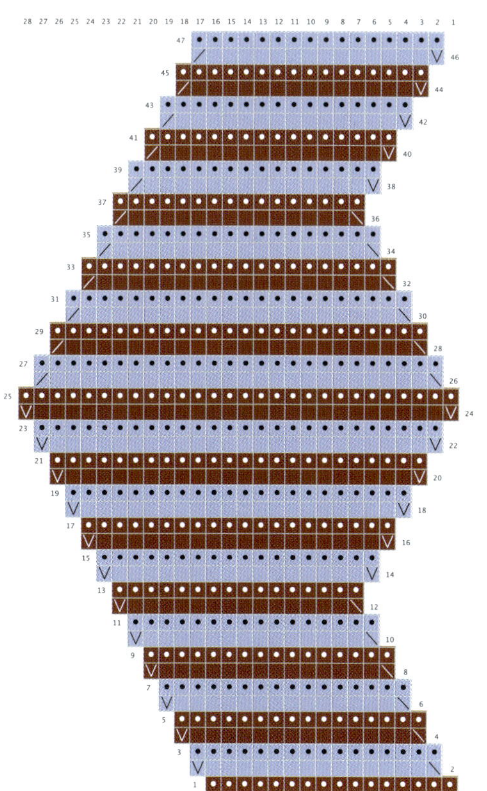

Knit—MC **dark brown**

Knit—CC **blue**

Knit on RS, purl on WS

Knit on WS, purl on RS

Kfb

Ssk

K2tog

BIRTA

Signý Benediktsdóttir (1900–1991) knitted these mittens and gave them to the Textile Museum. They have a horizontally striped cuff and a vertically striped palm. The back and the thumb are patterned with leaves, eight-petal roses, and diamonds. The originals were knitted in a dark brown main color and a white contrasting color. Pay close attention to the dominant color when knitting the stripes on the palm.

SIZE Women's medium

FINISHED MEASUREMENTS 11 in/28 cm long (incl. 3 in/7 cm ribbed cuff) and 7 in/18 cm around palm circumference.

YARN CYCA #1 (sock/fingering/baby) *Pirkkalanka Ohut* (100% wool, 437 yd/400 m / 100 g) Main color (MC): dark brown, 50 g. Contrasting color (CC): white, 50 g.

CYCA #1 (sock/fingering/baby) *Rowan Fine Tweed* (100% wool, 98 yd/90 m / 25 g) Main color (MC): dark blue, 50 g. Contrasting color (CC): light blue, 50 g.

Or similar fingering weight wool.

NEEDLES Size US 0/2 mm set of 5 DPNs for the cuff. Size US 1/2.5 mm set of 5 DPNs for the hand. Adjust needle size if necessary to obtain the correct gauge.

OTHER MATERIALS Scrap yarn and tapestry needle.

GAUGE 36 stitches and 36 rounds in stranded colorwork, on larger needles, after blocking = 4 in/10 cm.

If the gauge is not correct, the mittens might not fit properly.

PATTERN NOTES

- See the section beginning on page 30 for special techniques concerning yarn dominance, decreasing, increasing, and finishing.
- All stitches are knit stitches unless specifically noted otherwise.
- These mittens have a thumb gusset. The beginning of the gusset is marked with a yellow line on the chart where the separate thumb chart should be followed for the gusset.
- The chart is read from right to left. The thumb is worked at the beginning of the round on the right mitten and at the end of the round of the left mitten.

CUFF With smaller needles and MC, cast on 57 stitches. Arrange stitches on the needles: 12+15+15+15 stitches and join into round.

Work 27 rounds of k2, p1 ribbing (approximately 2 in/7 cm), following the instructions below for color changes:

Rounds 1–8: MC.

Rounds 9–10: CC.

Round 11: MC.

Round 12: CC.

Rounds 13–16: Repeat rounds 11–12 twice.

Round 17: MC.

Rounds 18–19: CC.

Rounds 20–27: MC.

HAND

Change to larger needles and knit 3 rounds with MC.

Work in pattern from the chart to round 31 where the increases start for the thumb—starting after the first stitch in the round on the right mitten and before second-last stitch on the left mitten. Follow the thumb chart when knitting the thumb gusset.

Knit the thumb increases while continuing with the body of the mitten—first the palm and then the back on the right mitten, and the back and then the palm on the left mitten.

THUMB INCREASES

Work the pattern from the chart and the increases for the thumb gusset *at the same time*.

Round 31: K1, M1R, k1, M1L, k55 = 59 stitches.

Rounds 32–33: Knit.

Round 34: K1, M1R, k3, M1L, k55 = 61 stitches.

Rounds 35–36: Knit.

Round 37: K1, M1R, k5, M1L, k55 = 63 stitches.

Rounds 38–39: Knit.

Round 40: K1, M1R, k7, M1L, k55 = 65 stitches.

Rounds 41–42: Knit.

Round 43: K1, M1R, k9, M1L, k55 = 67 stitches.

Rounds 44–45: Knit.

Round 46: K1, M1R, k11, M1L, k55 = 69 stitches.

Rounds 47–48: Knit.

Round 49: Work in pattern from the chart while working thumb openings.

RIGHT MITTEN K1, place the 13 thumb stitches onto scrap yarn and cast on 11 stitches at the back of the thumb in the appropriate color (blue line on the chart). Knit in pattern to the end of the round = 67 stitches.

LEFT MITTEN Knit until 14 stitches are left in the round. Place the 13 thumb stitches onto scrap yarn and cast on 11 stitches at the back of the thumb in the appropriate color (blue line on the chart). Knit in pattern to the end of the round = 67 stitches.

BOTH MITTENS Work in pattern from the chart to round 90.

START DECREASE ROUNDS Work in pattern from the chart while working decreases. Decrease 4 stitches on every round as follows:

RIGHT MITTEN **Note:** There is one extra stitch between decreases on the back of the mitten.

Round 90: K2, ssk, k25, k2tog, k4, ssk, k26, k2tog, k2 = 63 stitches.

Round 91: K2, ssk, k23, k2tog, k4, ssk, k24, k2tog, k2 = 59 stitches.

Round 92: K2, ssk, k21, k2tog, k4, ssk, k22, k2tog, k2 = 55 stitches.

Round 93: K2, ssk, k19, k2tog, k4, ssk, k20, k2tog, k2 = 51 stitches.

Round 94: K2, ssk, k17, k2tog, k4, ssk, k18, k2tog, k2 = 47 stitches.

Round 95: K2, ssk, k15, k2tog, k4, ssk, k16, k2tog, k2 = 43 stitches.

Round 96: K2, ssk, k13, k2tog, k4, ssk, k14, k2tog, k2 = 39 stitches.

Round 97: K2, ssk, k11, k2tog, k4, ssk, k12, k2tog, k2 = 35 stitches.

Round 98: K2, ssk, k9, k2tog, k4, ssk, k10, k2tog, k2 = 31 stitches.

Round 99: K2, ssk, k7, k2tog, k4, ssk, k8, k2tog, k2 = 27 stitches.

Round 100: K2, ssk, k5, k2tog, k4, ssk, k6, k2tog, k2 = 23 stitches.

Round 101: K2, ssk, k3, k2tog, k4, ssk, k4, k2tog, k2 = 19 stitches.

Round 102: K2, ssk, k1, k2tog, k4, ssk, k2, k2tog, k2 = 15 stitches.

Round 103: K2, sl1, k2tog, psso, k4, ssk, k2tog, k2 = 11 stitches.

LEFT MITTEN **Note:** There is one extra stitch between decreases on the back of the mitten.

Round 90: K2, ssk, k26, k2tog, k4, ssk, k25, k2tog, k2 = 63 stitches.

Round 91: K2, ssk, k24, k2tog, k4, ssk, k23, k2tog, k2 = 59 stitches.

Round 92: K2, ssk, k22, k2tog, k4, ssk, k21, k2tog, k2 = 55 stitches.

Round 93: K2, ssk, k20, k2tog, k4, ssk, k19, k2tog, k2 = 51 stitches.

Round 94: K2, ssk, k18, k2tog, k4, ssk, k17, k2tog, k2 = 47 stitches.

Round 95: K2, ssk, k16, k2tog, k4, ssk, k15, k2tog, k2 = 43 stitches.

Round 96: K2, ssk, k14, k2tog, k4, ssk, k13, k2tog, k2 = 39 stitches.

Round 97: K2, ssk, k12, k2tog, k4, ssk, k11, k2tog, k2 = 35 stitches.

Round 98: K2, ssk, k10, k2tog, k4, ssk, k9, k2tog, k2 = 31 stitches.

Round 99: K2, ssk, k8, k2tog, k4, ssk, k7, k2tog, k2 = 27 stitches.

Round 100: K2, ssk, k6, k2tog, k4, ssk, k5, k2tog, k2 = 23 stitches.

Round 101: K2, ssk, k4, k2tog, k4, ssk, k3, k2tog, k2 = 19 stitches.

Round 102: K2, ssk, k2, k2tog, k4, ssk, k1, k2tog, k2 = 15 stitches.

Round 103: K2, ssk, k2tog, k4, ssk, k2 = 11 stitches.

Close the top of the mitten (see the section about finishing, page 31).

THUMB

Remove scrap yarn, place stitches on 3 needles and knit around in pattern, picking up 2 stitches on either side of the opening and 11 stitches on the cast-on edge (red line on chart) = 28 stitches. Work in pattern from the chart and start decreasing on round 22.

Round 22: K1, ssk, k9, k2tog, k14 = 26 stitches.

Round 23: [K1, ssk, k7, k2tog, k1] x 2 = 22 stitches.

Round 24: [K1, ssk, k5, k2tog, k1] x 2 = 18 stitches.

Round 25: [K1, ssk, k3, k2tog, k1] x 2 = 14 stitches.

Round 26: [K1, ssk, k1, k2tog, k1] x 2 = 10 stitches

Round 27: [K1, ssk, k1] x 2 = 6 stitches.

Close the top of the thumb in the same way as the top of the mitten.

FINISHING

Weave in all ends. Wash and block both mittens, patting them gently to get the right size and to even out the stitches.

Left mitten

Right mitten

Thumb gusset and thumb

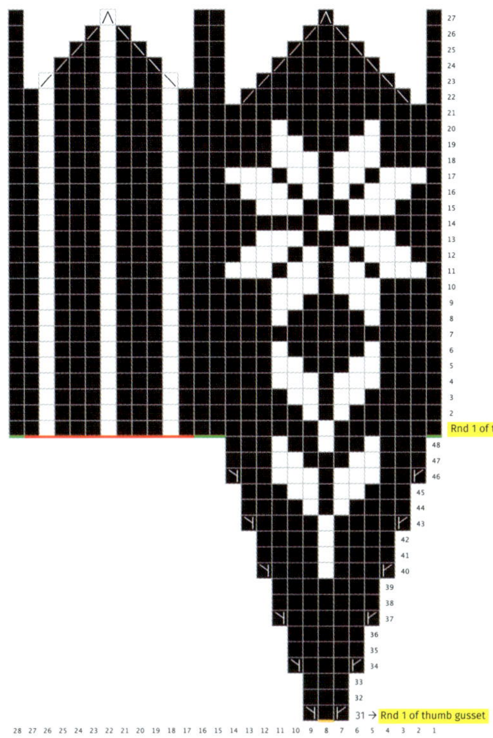

- Knit—MC **dark brown**
- Knit—CC **white**
- Purl
- M1R
- M1L
- K2tog
- Ssk
- Sl1, k2tog, psso
- Pick up and knit stitches behind the thumb
- CO stitches behind the thumb
- Start thumb gusset
- Pick up and knit stitches on either side of the thumb opening

TINNA

The West Fjords have their own unique mitten knitting tradition, which is said to date back to the latter half of the 19th century. Here is a good example from the Halldórustofa. The knitter is unknown; the wool is hand-spun, and was processed at Vigur in Ísafjarðardjúp. A short ribbed cuff is followed by a border, a single color on the body of the mitten, and another border on the top. It was also traditional to cast on with a different contrasting color, and knitters in this region kept a stash of brightly colored leftover yarn lengths for this purpose.

SIZE Women's medium

FINISHED MEASUREMENTS 10 in/25 cm long and 7 in/18 cm around palm circumference.

YARN CYCA #1 (sock/fingering/baby) *Pirkkalanka Ohut* (100% wool, 437 yd/400 m / 100 g) Main color (MC): white, 50 g. Contrasting color (CC): black, red, yellow, grey, green, 25 g of each.

CYCA #1 (sock/fingering/baby) *Rowan Fine Tweed* (100% wool, 98 yd/90 m / 25 g) Main color (MC): light brown, 50 g. Contrasting color (CC): dark brown, dark sea green, purple, pink, sea green, 25 g of each.

Or similar fingering weight wool.

NEEDLES Size US 0/2 mm set of 5 DPNs for the single-color sections. Size US 1/2.5 mm set of 5 DPNs for the colorwork. Adjust needle size if necessary to obtain the correct gauge.

OTHER MATERIALS Scrap yarn and tapestry needle.

GAUGE Single-color knitting: 34 stitches and 42 rounds in stockinette stitch, on smaller needles, after blocking = 4 in/10 cm.

Stranded knitting: 36 stitches and 42 rounds in stranded colorwork, on larger needles, after blocking = 4 in/10 cm.

If the gauge is not correct, the mittens might not fit properly.

PATTERN NOTES

- See the section beginning on page 30 for special techniques concerning yarn dominance, decreasing, increasing, and finishing.
- All stitches are knit stitches unless specifically noted otherwise.
- Both mittens are knitted from the same chart.
- Read all chart rounds from right to left.
- The thumb is worked at the beginning of the round on the right mitten and at the end of the round on the left mitten.
- Some knitters knit tighter when knitting stranded colorwork. So it may be necessary to change needle sizes between single-color and stranded knitting in order to maintain gauge.

CUFF

With smaller needles and grey yarn, cast on 60 stitches using the long-tail cast-on method (see the section about cast-ons, page 28, for other methods). Arrange stitches evenly on the needles (15 stitches on each needle) and join into round.

With black yarn, work 8 rounds of ribbing: k2, p1.

Change to larger needles. Work in stripes and stranded colorwork following the chart until round 14.

HAND

Round 14, inc. round: [K14, kfb] x 4 = 64 stitches.

With 16 stitches on each needle, work from the chart. Finish the first part of the stranded chart and then knit with MC and smaller needles to the thumb opening at round 48.

Round 48: Work the thumb openings as follows:

RIGHT MITTEN

K1, k11 stitches with scrap yarn (green line on the chart), slip these 11 stitches back onto left needle and knit in pattern to the end of round.

LEFT MITTEN

Knit until 13 stitches are left in the round. K11 stitches with scrap yarn (red line on the chart), slip these 11 stitches back onto left needle and knit in pattern to the end of the round.

Knit with MC until round 75 is reached. Then switch to larger needles and knit according to the chart until the 91st round is reached and decreasing starts.

START DECREASE ROUNDS

Work in pattern from the chart while working decreases. Decrease 4 stitches on indicated rounds as follows:

Round 91: [Ssk, k28, k2tog] x 2 = 60 stitches.

Rounds 92, 94, 96, 98, 100, and 102: Knit.

Round 93: [Ssk, k26, k2tog] x 2 = 56 stitches.

Round 95: [Ssk, k24, k2tog] x 2 = 52 stitches.

Round 97: [Ssk, k22, k2tog] x 2 = 48 stitches.

Round 99: [Ssk, k20, k2tog] x 2 = 44 stitches.

Round 101: [Ssk, k18, k2tog] x 2 = 40 stitches.

Round 103: [Ssk, k16, k2tog] x 2 = 36 stitches.

Round 104: [Ssk, k14, k2tog] x 2 = 32 stitches.

Round 105: [Ssk, k12, k2tog] x 2 = 28 stitches.

Round 106: [Ssk, k10, k2tog] x 2 = 24 stitches.

Round 107: [Ssk, k8, k2tog] x 2 = 20 stitches.

Round 108: [Ssk, k6, k2tog] x 2 = 16 stitches.

Round 109: [Ssk, k4, k2tog] x 2 = 12 stitches.

Round 110: [Ssk, k2, k2tog] x 2 = 8 stitches.

Close the top of the mitten (see the section about finishing, page 31).

THUMB

Remove scrap yarn, place stitches on 3 smaller needles and knit around in pattern, picking up 2 stitches on either side of the opening and one extra stitch at the top of the opening = 26 stitches. Work in MC to round 18, then switch to larger needles and continue in pattern from the chart to round 22.

START DECREASE

Round 22: [K4, k2tog, k5, k2tog] x 2 = 22 stitches.

Rounds 23, 25, and 27: Knit.

Round 24: [K3, k2tog, k4, k2tog] x 2 = 18 stitches.

Round 26: [K2, k2tog, k3, k2tog] x 2 = 14 stitches.

Round 28: [K1, k2tog, k2, k2tog] x 2 = 10 stitches.

Round 29: [K3, k2tog] x 2 = 8 stitches.

Round 30: [K2tog] x 4 = 4 stitches.

Close the top of the thumb in the same way as the top of the mitten.

FINISHING

Weave in all ends. Wash and block both mittens, patting them gently to get the right size and to even out the stitches.

Left and right mittens

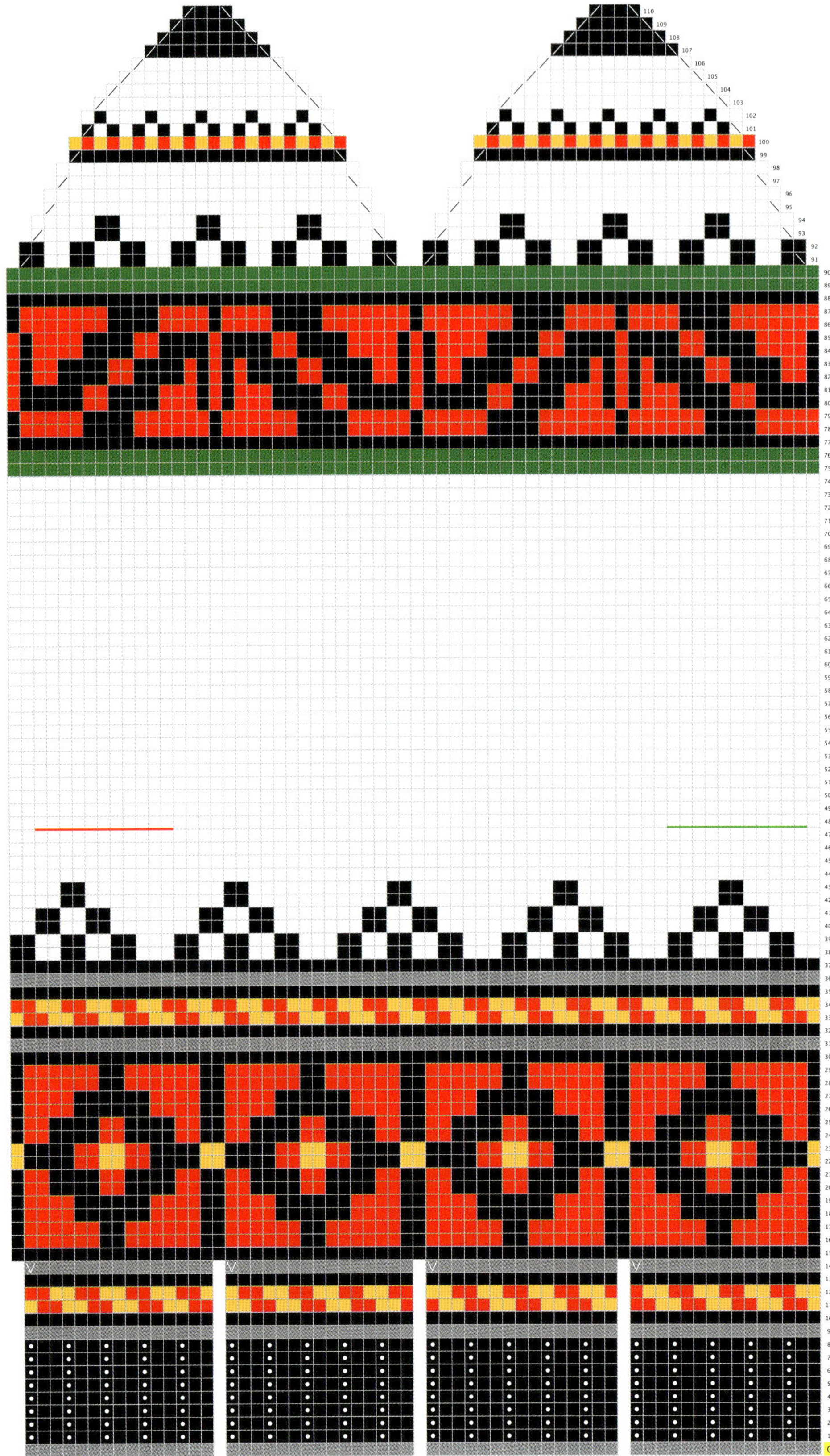

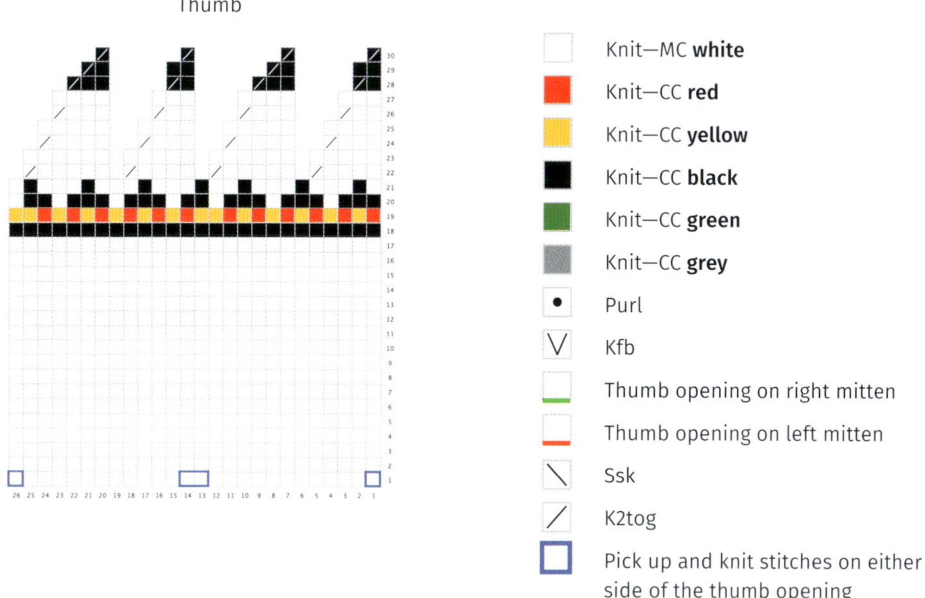
Thumb
Knit—MC white
Knit—CC red
Knit—CC yellow
Knit—CC black
Knit—CC green
Knit—CC grey
Purl
Kfb
Thumb opening on right mitten
Thumb opening on left mitten
Ssk
K2tog
Pick up and knit stitches on either side of the thumb opening

SALKA

These very stylistically minimalist and elegant mittens are preserved in the Textile Museum. The knitter remains unknown, but the mittens seem to have been knitted for very slender hands. They are knitted with two colors: natural black as the main color, and white as the contrast color. The cuff starts with purl rounds and then the rest of the mitten is knitted in stocking stitch. The thumb is picked up and knitted afterwards. The main pattern is an easily memorized one.

SIZE Women's medium

FINISHED MEASUREMENTS 11 in/27.5 cm long and 7 in/18 cm around palm circumference.

YARN CYCA #1 (sock/fingering/baby) *Pirkkalanka Ohut* (100% wool, 437 yd/400 m / 100 g)
Main color (MC): dark brown, 50 g. Contrasting color (CC): white, 50 g.

CYCA #1 (sock/fingering/baby) *Rowan Fine Tweed* (100% wool, 98 yd/90 m / 25 g)
Main color (MC): dark blue, 50 g. Contrasting color (CC): rust red, 50 g.

Or similar fingering weight wool.

NEEDLES Size US 0/2 mm set of 5 DPNs for the cuff. Size US 1/2.5 mm set of 5 DPNs for the hand. Adjust needle size if necessary to obtain the correct gauge.

OTHER MATERIALS Scrap yarn and tapestry needle.

GAUGE 36 stitches and 38 rounds in stranded colorwork on larger needles, after blocking = 4 in/10 cm.

If the gauge is not correct, the mittens might not fit properly.

PATTERN NOTES

- See the section beginning on page 30 for special techniques concerning yarn dominance, decreasing, increasing, and finishing.
- All stitches are knit stitches unless specifically noted otherwise.
- Both mittens are knitted from the same chart.
- Read all chart rounds from right to left.
- The thumb is worked at the beginning of the round on the right mitten and at the end of the round on the left mitten.

CUFF With smaller needles and MC, cast on 64 stitches using the twisted German cast-on (see the section about cast-ons, page 28). Arrange stitches evenly on the needles and join into round.

Purl 2 rounds.

Rounds 3–30: Work from chart.

HAND

Change to larger needles. Work in pattern from the chart to round 50.

Round 50: Work in pattern from the chart while working thumb openings:

RIGHT MITTEN

K2, k11 stitches with scrap yarn (green line on the chart), slip these 11 stitches back onto left needle and knit in pattern to the end of the round.

LEFT MITTEN

Knit until 14 stitches are left in the round. K11 stitches with scrap yarn (red line on the chart), slip these 11 stitches back onto left needle and knit in pattern to the end of the round.

BOTH MITTENS

Work in pattern from the chart to round 87.

START DECREASE ROUNDS

Work in pattern from the chart while working decreases.

The last stitch on needle 2 and the last stitch on needle 4 will form a straight line to the top of the mitten.

Decrease 4 stitches on the indicated rounds as follows:

Round 87: [Ssk, k27, k2tog, k1] x 2 = 60 stitches.

Rounds 88, 90, 92, 94, and 96: Knit.

Round 89: [Ssk, k25, k2tog, k1] x 2 = 56 stitches.

Round 91: [Ssk, k23, k2tog, k1] x 2 = 52 stitches.

Round 93: [Ssk, k21, k2tog, k1] x 2 = 48 stitches.

Round 95: [Ssk, k19, k2tog, k1] x 2 = 44 stitches.

Round 97: [Ssk, k17, k2tog, k1] x 2 = 40 stitches.

Round 98: [Ssk, k15, k2tog, k1] x 2 = 36 stitches.

Round 99: [Ssk, k13, k2tog, k1] x 2 = 32 stitches.

Round 100: [Ssk, k11, k2tog, k1] x 2 = 28 stitches.

Round 101: [Ssk, k9, k2tog, k1] x 2 = 24 stitches.

Round 102: [Ssk, k7, k2tog, k1] x 2 = 20 stitches.

Round 103: [Ssk, k5, k2tog, k1] x 2 = 16 stitches.

Round 104: [Ssk, k3, k2tog, k1] x 2 = 12 stitches.

Round 105: [Ssk, k1, k2tog, k1] x 2 = 8 stitches.

Close the top of the mitten (see the section about finishing, page 31).

THUMB

Remove scrap yarn, place stitches on 3 needles and knit around in pattern, picking up 3 stitches on either side of the opening and one extra stitch at the top of the opening = 28 stitches. Work in pattern from the chart and start decreasing on round 21.

Round 21: [Ssk, k9, k2tog, k1] x 2 = 24 stitches.

Rounds 22 and 24: Knit.

Round 23: [Ssk, k7, k2tog, k1] x 2 = 20 stitches.

Round 25: [Ssk, k5, k2tog, k1] x 2 = 16 stitches.

Round 26: [Ssk, k3, k2tog, k1] x 2 = 12 stitches.

Round 27: [Ssk, k1, k2tog, k1] x 2 = 8 stitches.

Round 28: [Ssk, k2] x 2 = 6 stitches.

Close the top of the thumb in the same way as the top of the mitten.

FINISHING

Weave in all ends. Wash and block both mittens, patting them gently to get the right size and to even out the stitches.

Left and right mittens

Thumb

- Knit—MC **dark brown**
- Knit—CC **white**
- Purl
- Thumb opening on right mitten
- Thumb opening on left mitten
- K2tog
- Ssk
- Pick up and knit stitches on either side of the thumb opening

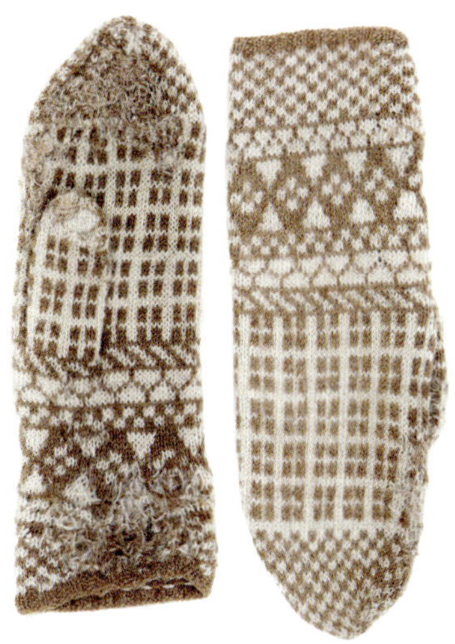

HARPA

These mittens are from Halldórustofa. In 1962, Halldóra Bjarnadóttir gave these mittens to the Farmers Association of Iceland, and they later went to the museum in 2003. These mittens are knitted in 2-ply hand-spun wool. They show signs of extensive use and wear in places, and are heavily darned and mended. The cuff is worked with 4 rounds of ribbing followed by various patterns, and with an afterthought thumb. This is a decorative and multi-patterned mitten that is an exciting project for those new to stranded knitting.

SIZE Women's medium

FINISHED MEASUREMENTS 11 in/27.5 cm long and 7.5 in/19 cm around palm circumference.

YARN CYCA #1 (sock/fingering/baby) *Pirkkalanka Ohut* (100% wool, 437 yd/400 m / 100 g) Main color (MC): white, 50 g. Contrasting color (CC): light brown, 50 g.

CYCA #1 (sock/fingering/baby) *Rowan Fine Tweed* (100% wool, 98 yd/90 m / 25 g) Main color (MC): yellow, 50 g. Contrasting color (CC): burgundy, 50 g.

Or similar fingering weight wool.

NEEDLES Size US 0/2 mm set of 5 DPNs for the cuff. Size US 1/2.5 mm set of 5 DPNs for the hand. Adjust needle size if necessary to obtain the correct gauge.

OTHER MATERIALS Scrap yarn and tapestry needle.

GAUGE 38 stitches and 38 rounds in stranded colorwork, on larger needles, after blocking = 4 in/10 cm.

If the gauge is not correct, the mittens might not fit properly.

PATTERN NOTES

- See the section beginning on page 30 for special techniques concerning yarn dominance, decreasing, increasing, and finishing.
- All stitches are knit stitches unless specifically noted otherwise.
- Both mittens are knitted from the same chart.
- Read all chart rounds from right to left.
- The thumb is worked at the beginning of the round on the right mitten and at the end of the round on the left mitten.

CUFF With smaller needles and MC, cast on 72 stitches. Arrange stitches on the needles: 20+16+20+16 stitches and join into round.

Work 4 rounds (0.5 in/1 cm) of ribbing: k2, p2.

HAND Change to larger needles. Rearrange stitches so there are 18 stitches on each of the 4 needles. Work in pattern from the chart to round 48.

Round 48: Work in pattern from the chart while working thumb openings:

RIGHT MITTEN K2, k12 stitches with scrap yarn (green line on the chart), slip these 12 stitches back onto left needle and knit in pattern to the end of the round.

LEFT MITTEN Knit until 13 stitches are left in the round. K12 stitches with scrap yarn (red line on the chart), slip these 12 stitches back onto left needle and knit in pattern to the end of the round.

BOTH MITTENS Work in pattern from the chart to round 89.

START DECREASE ROUNDS Work in pattern from the chart while working decreases. Decrease 4 stitches on every round as follows:

Round 89: [K1, ssk, k31, k2tog] x 2 = 68 stitches.

Round 90: [K1, ssk, k29, k2tog] x 2 = 64 stitches.

Round 91: [K1, ssk, k27, k2tog] x 2 = 60 stitches.

Round 92: [K1, ssk, k25, k2tog] x 2 = 56 stitches.

Round 93: [K1, ssk, k23, k2tog] x 2 = 52 stitches.

Round 94: [K1, ssk, k21, k2tog] x 2 = 48 stitches.

Round 95: [K1, ssk, k19, k2tog] x 2 = 44 stitches.

Round 96: [K1, ssk, k17, k2tog] x 2 = 40 stitches.

Round 97: [K1, ssk, k15, k2tog] x 2 = 36 stitches.

Round 98: [K1, ssk, k13, k2tog] x 2 = 32 stitches.

Round 99: [K1, ssk, k11, k2tog] x 2 = 28 stitches.

Round 100: [K1, ssk, k9, k2tog] x 2 = 24 stitches.

Round 101: [K1, ssk, k7, k2tog] x 2 = 20 stitches.

Round 102: [K1, ssk, k5, k2tog] x 2 = 16 stitches.

Round 103: [K1, ssk, k3, k2tog] x 2 = 12 stitches.

Round 104: [K1, ssk, k1, k2tog] x 2 = 8 stitches.

Close the top of the mitten (see the section about finishing, page 31).

THUMB

Remove scrap yarn, place stitches on 3 needles and knit around in pattern, picking up 2 stitches on either side of the opening and one extra stitch at the top of the opening = 28 stitches. Work in pattern from the chart and start decreasing on round 21.

Round 21: [K1, ssk, k8, k2tog, k1] x 2 = 24 stitches.

Round 22: [K1, ssk, k6, k2tog, k1] x 2 = 20 stitches.

Round 23: [K1, ssk, k4, k2tog, k1] x 2 = 16 stitches.

Round 24: [K1, ssk, k2, k2tog, k1] x 2 = 12 stitches.

Round 25: [K1, ssk, k2tog, k1] x 2 = 8 stitches.

Close the top of the thumb in the same way as the top of the mitten.

FINISHING

Weave in all ends. Wash and block both mittens, patting them gently to get the right size and to even out the stitches.

Left and right mittens

Thumb

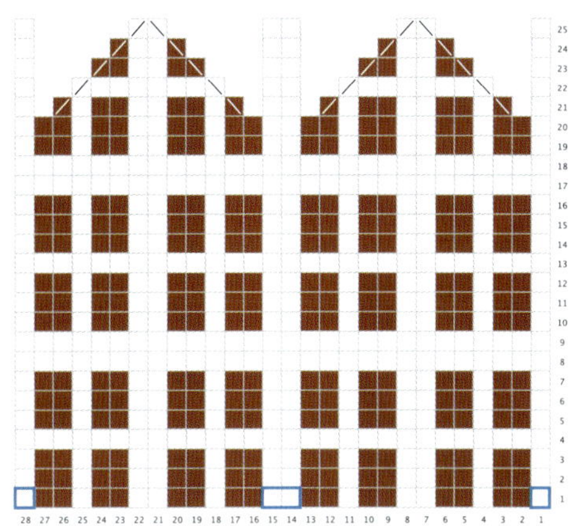

(white square)	Knit—MC **white**
(brown square)	Knit—CC **light brown**
•	Purl
/	K2tog
\	Ssk
(red line)	Thumb opening on left mitten
(green line)	Thumb opening on right mitten
(blue square)	Pick up and knit stitches on either side of the thumb opening

HREFNA

Sigríður Björnsdóttir (1897–1990) from Kornsá knitted these mittens from delicate homespun wool. The main color is black, with small patterns of white eight-petal roses. The original mittens are tightly knitted, with a small gauge. The pattern is a simple variation on the very popular eight-petal rose, and well suited for adding more colors. The instructions are not complicated, but some practice in stranded knitting is useful before embarking on a pair of your own.

SIZE Women's medium

FINISHED MEASUREMENTS 11 in/28 cm long (incl. 3 in/7 cm ribbed cuff) and 7 in/18 cm around palm circumference.

This pattern can be adapted for the use of as many colors as you want.

YARN CYCA #1 (sock/fingering/baby) *Pirkkalanka Ohut* (100% wool, 437 yd/400 m / 100 g) Main color (MC): black, 50 g. Contrasting color (CC): white or light grey, 50 g.

CYCA #1 (sock/fingering/baby) *Rowan Fine Tweed* (100% wool, 98 yd/90 m / 25 g) Main color (MC): burgundy, 50 g. Contrasting colors (CC): carmine, pink, orange, yellow, 25 g of each.

Or similar fingering weight wool.

NEEDLES Size US 0/2 mm set of 5 DPNs for the cuff. Size US 1/2.5 mm set of 5 DPNs for the hand. Adjust needle size if necessary to obtain the correct gauge.

OTHER MATERIALS Scrap yarn and tapestry needle.

GAUGE 36 stitches and 34 rounds in stranded colorwork, on larger needles, after blocking = 4 in/10 cm.

If the gauge is not correct, the mittens might not fit properly.

PATTERN NOTES

- See the section beginning on page 30 for special techniques concerning yarn dominance, decreasing, increasing, and finishing.
- All stitches are knit stitches unless specifically noted otherwise.
- Both mittens are knitted from the same chart.
- Read all chart rounds from right to left.
- The thumb is worked at the beginning of the round on the right mitten and at the end of the round on the left mitten.

CUFF With smaller needles and MC, cast on 60 stitches. Arrange stitches on the needles: 16+16+16+12 stitches and join into round.

Work 24 rounds (3 in/7 cm) of ribbing: k2, p2.

HAND Change to larger needles.

Round 25, inc. round: [K15, M1L] x 4 = 64 stitches.

Rearrange stitches so there are 16 stitches on each of the four needles. Work in pattern from the chart to round 42.

Round 42: Work in pattern from the chart while working thumb openings:

RIGHT MITTEN K2, k13 stitches with scrap yarn (yellow line on the chart), slip these 13 stitches back onto left needle and knit in pattern to the end of the round.

LEFT MITTEN Knit until 14 stitches are left in the round. K13 stitches with scrap yarn (red line on the chart), slip these 13 stitches back onto left needle and knit in pattern to the end of the round.

BOTH MITTENS Work in pattern from the chart to round 84.

START DECREASE ROUNDS Work in pattern from the chart while working decreases.
Decrease 4 stitches on every round as follows:

Round 84: [K1, ssk, k27, k2tog] x 2 = 60 stitches.

Round 85: [K1, ssk, k25, k2tog] x 2 = 56 stitches.

Round 86: [K1, ssk, k23, k2tog] x 2 = 52 stitches.

Round 87: [K1, ssk, k21, k2tog] x 2 = 48 stitches.

Round 88: [K1, ssk, k19, k2tog] x 2 = 44 stitches.

Round 89: [K1, ssk, k17, k2tog] x 2 = 40 stitches.

Round 90: [K1, ssk, k15, k2tog] x 2 = 36 stitches.

Round 91: [K1, ssk, k13, k2tog] x 2 = 32 stitches.

Round 92: [K1, ssk, k11, k2tog] x 2 = 28 stitches.

Round 93: [K1, ssk, k9, k2tog] x 2 = 24 stitches.

Round 94: [K1, ssk, k7, k2tog] x 2 = 20 stitches.

Round 95: [K1, ssk, k5, k2tog] x 2 = 16 stitches.

Round 96: [K1, ssk, k3, k2tog] x 2 = 12 stitches.

Round 97: [K1, ssk, k1, k2tog] x 2 = 8 stitches.

Close the top of the mitten (see the section about finishing, page 31).

THUMB

Remove scrap yarn, place stitches on 3 needles and knit around in pattern, picking up 2 stitches on either side of the opening and one extra stitch at the top of the opening = 30 stitches. Work in pattern from the chart and start decreasing on round 19.

Round 19: [Ssk, k5, ssk, k6] x 2 = 26 stitches.

Round 20: [Ssk, k4, ssk, k5] x 2 = 22 stitches.

Round 21: [Ssk, k3, ssk, k4] x 2 = 18 stitches.

Round 22: [Ssk, k2, ssk, k3] x 2 = 14 stitches.

Round 23: [Ssk, k1, ssk, k2] x 2 = 10 stitches.

Round 24: [Ssk twice, k1] x 2 = 6 stitches.

Round 25: [K1, ssk] x 2 = 4 stitches.

Close the top of the thumb in the same way as the top of the mitten.

FINISHING

Weave in all ends. Wash and block both mittens, patting them gently to get the right size and to even out the stitches.

Left and right mittens

Thumb

Knit—MC **burgundy**
Knit—CC **carmine**
Knit—CC **pink**
Knit—CC **orange**
Knit—CC **yellow**
Purl
M1L
Ssk
K2tog
Thumb opening on right mitten
Thumb opening on left mitten
Pick up and knit stitches on either side of the thumb opening

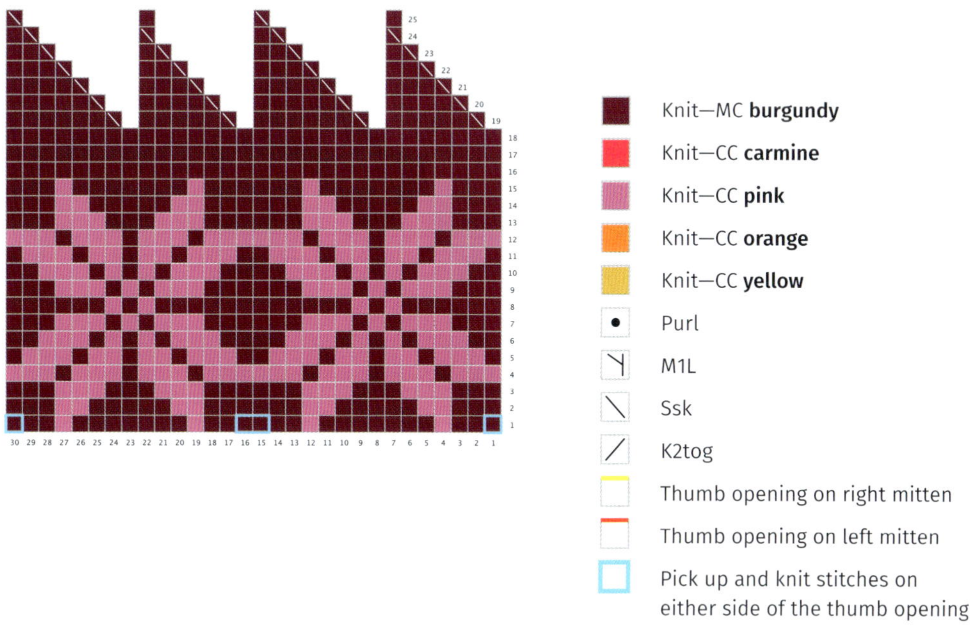

EDDA

The influence of Norwegian Selbu rose mittens very likely spread to Iceland at some point. But Icelandic knitters also derived their own versions of the eight-petal rose pattern in many different ways. Here is a pair by an unknown knitter with dark brown as the main color and white used as the contrasting color. White is used for stripes in the cuff as well as a band of pattern just above the cuff. The palm of the mitten is then patterned with vertical stripes and the back of the mitten with eight-petal roses. The patterned thumbs are knitted with a gusset. A project for those who want to tackle the classic patterns and thumb gusset.

SIZE Women's medium

FINISHED MEASUREMENTS 11.5 in/29 cm long (incl. 3 in/7 cm ribbed cuff) and 7 in/18 cm around palm circumference.

YARN CYCA #1 (sock/fingering/baby) *Pirkkalanka Ohut* (100% wool, 437 yd/400 m / 100 g) Main color (MC): dark brown, 50 g. Contrasting color (CC): white, 50 g.

CYCA #1 (sock/fingering/baby) *Rowan Fine Tweed* (100% wool, 98 yd/90 m / 25 g) Main color (MC): orange, 50 g. Contrasting color (CC): dark grey, 25 g.

Or similar fingering weight wool.

NEEDLES Size US 0/2 mm set of 5 DPNs for the cuff. Size US 1/2.5 mm set of 5 DPNs for the hand. Adjust needle size if necessary to obtain the correct gauge.

OTHER MATERIALS Scrap yarn and tapestry needle.

GAUGE 36 stitches and 36 rounds in stranded colorwork, on larger needles after blocking = 4 in/10 cm.

If the gauge is not correct, the mittens might not fit properly.

PATTERN NOTES

- See the section beginning on page 30 for special techniques concerning yarn dominance, decreasing, increasing, and finishing.
- All stitches are knit stitches unless specifically noted otherwise.
- These mittens have a thumb gusset. The beginning of the pattern for the gusset is marked with a blue line.
- The chart is read from right to left.
- The thumb is worked at the beginning of the round on the right mitten and at the end of the round on the left mitten.

RIGHT MITTEN With smaller needles and MC, cast on 60 stitches. Arrange stitches evenly on the needles and join into round. Work 25 rounds (3 in/7 cm) of k2, p1 ribbing, following the instructions below for color changes:

Rounds 1–11: MC.

Round 12: CC.

Round 13: MC.

Round 14: CC.

Round 15: MC.

Round 16: CC.

Rounds 17–25: MC.

HAND

Change to larger needles. Work in pattern from the chart to round 35 where the increases start for the thumb—starting after the first stitch in the round on the right mitten and before the second-last stitch on the left mitten. While knitting the thumb increases, continue with the body of the mitten—first the palm and then the back on the right mitten, and the back and then the palm on the left mitten.**

THUMB GUSSET

Work the pattern from the chart and the increases for the thumb gusset *at the same time.*

Round 35: K1, M1R, k1, M1L, k58 = 62 stitches.

Rounds 36–37: Knit.

Round 38: K1, M1R, k3, M1L, k58 = 64 stitches.

Rounds 39–40: Knit.

Round 41: K1, M1R, k5, M1L, k58 = 66 stitches.

Rounds 42–43: Knit.

Round 44: K1, M1R, k7, M1L, k58 = 68 stitches.

Rounds 45–46: Knit.

Round 47: K1, M1R, k9, M1L, k58 = 70 stitches.***

Rounds 48–52: Knit.

Round 53: Knit in pattern to the thumb stitches (black line on the chart).

Place the 11 thumb stitches onto scrap yarn and cast on 11 stitches. Knit in pattern to the end of the round = 70 stitches.

Work in pattern from the chart to round 91.

START DECREASE ROUNDS

Work in pattern from the chart while working decreases. The decreases at the top of the mitten are worked twice in the first two rounds and thereafter 4 times a round.

Round 91: K1, ssk, k31, k2tog, k34 = 68 stitches.

Round 92: K1, ssk, k29, k2tog, k34 = 66 stitches.****

Round 93: [K1, ssk, k27, k2tog, k1] x 2 = 62 stitches.

Round 94: [K1, ssk, k25, k2tog, k1] x 2 = 58 stitches.

Round 95: [K1, ssk, k23, k2tog, k1] x 2 = 54 stitches.

Round 96: [K1, ssk, k21, k2tog, k1] x 2 = 50 stitches.

Round 97: [K1, ssk, k19, k2tog, k1] x 2 = 46 stitches.

Round 98: [K1, ssk, k17, k2tog, k1] x 2 = 42 stitches.

Round 99: [K1, ssk, k15, k2tog, k1] x 2 = 38 stitches.

Round 100: [K1, ssk, k13, k2tog, k1] x 2 = 34 stitches.

Round 101: [K1, ssk, k11, k2tog, k1] x 2 = 30 stitches.

Round 102: [K1, ssk, k9, k2tog, k1] x 2 = 26 stitches.

Round 103: [K1, ssk, k7, k2tog, k1] x 2 = 22 stitches.

Round 104: [K1, ssk, k5, k2tog, k1] x 2 = 18 stitches.

Round 105: [K1, ssk, k3, k2tog, k1] x 2 = 14 stitches.

Round 106: [K1, ssk, k1, k2tog, k1] x 2 = 10 stitches.

Close the top of the mitten (see the section about finishing, page 31).

LEFT MITTEN

Work as right mitten to **.

THUMB GUSSET

Work the pattern from the chart and the increases for the thumb gusset *at the same time*.

Round 35: K58, M1R, k1, M1L, k1 = 62 stitches.

Rounds 36–37: Knit.

Round 38: K58, M1R, k3, M1L, k1 = 64 stitches.

Rounds 39–40: Knit.

Round 41: K58, M1R, k5, M1L, k1 = 66 stitches.

Rounds 42–43: Knit.

Round 44: K58, M1R, k7, M1L, k1 = 68 stitches.

Rounds 45–46: Knit.

Round 47: K58, M1R, k9, M1L, k1 = 70 stitches.

START DECREASE ROUNDS

Knit as right mitten from *** to decreases.

Work in pattern from the chart while working decreases. The decreases are worked twice in the first two rounds and thereafter 4 times a round.

Round 91: K34, ssk, k31, k2tog, k1 = 68 stitches.

Round 92: K34, ssk, k29, k2tog, k1 = 66 stitches.

BOTH THUMBS

Knit as right mitten from ****.

Remove scrap yarn, place stitches on 3 needles and knit around in pattern, picking up 2 stitches on either side of the opening and 11 stitches on the cast-on edge = 26 stitches. Work in pattern from the chart and start decreasing on round 21.

Round 21: [K1, ssk, k7, k2tog, k1] x 2 = 22 stitches.

Round 22: [K1, ssk, k5, k2tog, k1] x 2 = 18 stitches.

Round 23: [K1, ssk, k3, k2tog, k1] x 2 = 14 stitches.

Round 24: [K1, ssk, k1, k2tog, k1] x 2 = 10 stitches.

Round 25: [K1, sl1, k2tog, psso, k1] x 2 = 6 stitches.

Close the top of the thumb in the same way as the top of the mitten.

FINISHING

Weave in all ends. Wash and block both mittens, patting them gently to get the right size and to even out the stitches.

Left mitten

Right mitten

Thumb

25 24 23 22 21 20 19 18 17 16 15 14 13 12 11 10 9 8 7 6 5 4 3 2 1
26 25 24 23 22 21 20 19 18 17 16 15 14 13 12 11 10 9 8 7 6 5 4 3 2 1

Knit—MC **orange**
Knit—CC **dark grey**
Purl
Ssk
K2tog
M1R
M1L
Sl1, k2tog, psso
Thumb opening
Start thumb gusset
Pick up and knit stitches on either side of the thumb opening

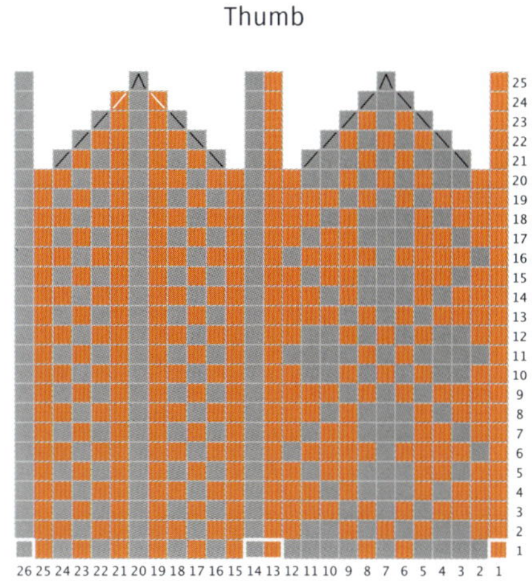

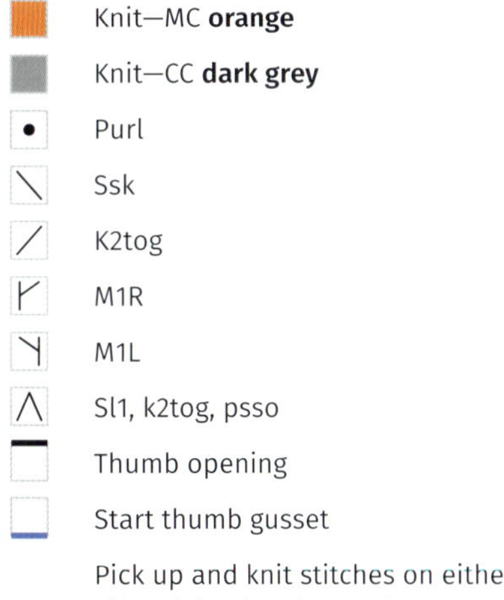

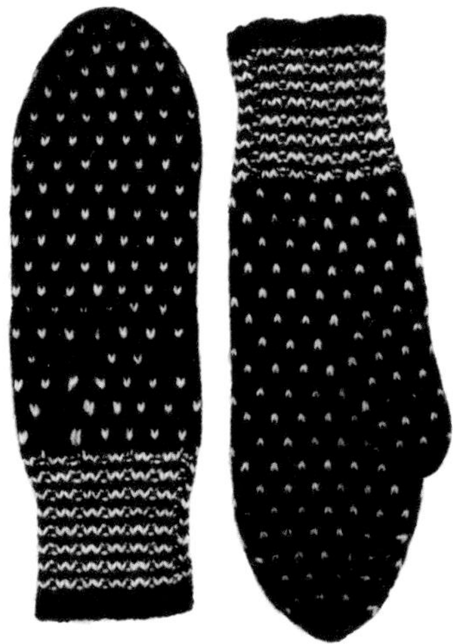

LILJA

Anna Gísladóttir (1906–1993) from Saurbær in Vatnsdalur knitted these simple but stylish mittens, which were donated to the Textile Museum in 2002. They are knitted in black wool as the main color with a white contrasting wool for the stripes in the cuff and the dots in the main body of the mittens. They are relatively simple to knit, but were chosen for this book because they're a great exercise in using a dominant color in a one-stitch pattern sequence.

SIZE Women's medium

FINISHED MEASUREMENTS 11 in/28 cm long (incl. 3 in/8 cm ribbed cuff) and 7 in/18 cm around palm circumference.

YARN CYCA #1 (sock/fingering/baby) *Pirkkalanka Ohut* (100% wool, 437 yd/400 m / 100 g)
Main color (MC): black, 50 g. Contrasting color (CC): white, 50 g.

CYCA #2 (sport/baby) *Mohair by Canard Kid Mohair 2-ply* (65% Mohair, 35% Merino, 193 yd/176 m / 50 g)
Main color (MC): light grey, 50 g. Contrasting color (CC): blue green, 50 g.

Or similar fingering weight wool.

NEEDLES Size US 0/2 mm set of 5 DPNs for the cuff. Size US 1/2.5 mm set of 5 DPNs for the hand. Adjust needle size if necessary to obtain the correct gauge.

OTHER MATERIALS Scrap yarn and tapestry needle.

GAUGE 38 stitches and 38 rounds in stranded colorwork, on larger needles, after blocking = 4 in/10 cm.

If the gauge is not correct, the mittens might not fit properly.

PATTERN NOTES

- See the section beginning on page 30 for special techniques concerning yarn dominance, decreasing, increasing, and finishing.
- All stitches are knit stitches unless specifically noted otherwise.
- Both mittens are knitted from the same chart.
- Read all chart rounds from right to left.
- The thumb is worked at the beginning of the round on the right mitten and at the end of the round on the left mitten.

CUFF With smaller needles and MC, cast on 64 stitches. Arrange stitches evenly on the needles and join into round.

Work 28 rounds (3 in/8 cm) of k2, p2 ribbing, following the instructions below for color changes:

Work 6 rounds with MC and then work the striped pattern into the ribbed cuffs: [1 round CC, 2 rounds MC] x 7 and then one final ribbing round in MC.

HAND

Change to larger needles.

Round 29, inc. round: [K16, M1L] x 4 = 68 stitches.

Work in pattern from the chart to round 54.

Round 54: Work in pattern from the chart while working thumb openings:

RIGHT MITTEN

K2, k12 stitches with scrap yarn (green line on the chart), slip these 12 stitches back onto left needle and knit in pattern to the end of the round.

LEFT MITTEN

Knit until 14 stitches are left in the round. K12 stitches with scrap yarn (red line on the chart), slip these 12 stitches back onto left needle and knit in pattern to the end of the round.

BOTH MITTENS

Work in pattern from the chart to round 85 (or when the top of the little finger has been reached).

START DECREASE ROUNDS

Work in pattern from the chart while working decreases.
Decrease 4 stitches on every round as follows:

Round 85: [K1, ssk, k28, k2tog, k1] x 2 = 64 stitches.

Rounds 86, 88, 90, 92, 94, 96, and 98: Knit.

Round 87: [K1, ssk, k26, k2tog, k1] x 2 = 60 stitches.

Round 89: [K1, ssk, k24, k2tog, k1] x 2 = 56 stitches.

Round 91: [K1, ssk, k22, k2tog, k1] x 2 = 52 stitches.

Round 93: [K1, ssk, k20, k2tog, k1] x 2 = 48 stitches.

Round 95: [K1, ssk, k18, k2tog, k1] x 2 = 44 stitches.

Round 97: [K1, ssk, k16, k2tog, k1] x 2 = 40 stitches.

Round 99: [K1, ssk, k14, k2tog, k1] x 2 = 36 stitches.

Round 100: [K1, ssk, k12, k2tog, k1] x 2 = 32 stitches.

Round 101: [K1, ssk, k10, k2tog, k1] x 2 = 28 stitches.

Round 102: [K1, ssk, k8, k2tog, k1] x 2 = 24 stitches.

Round 103: [K1, ssk, k6, k2tog, k1] x 2 = 20 stitches.

Round 104: [K1, ssk, k4, k2tog, k1] x 2 = 16 stitches.

Round 105: [K1, ssk, k2, k2tog, k1] x 2 = 12 stitches.

Round 106: [K1, ssk, k2tog, k1] x 2 = 8 stitches.

Close the top of the mitten (see the section about finishing, page 31).

THUMB

Remove scrap yarn, place stitches on 3 needles and knit around in pattern, picking up 2 stitches on either side of the opening and one extra stitch at the top of the opening = 28 stitches. Work in pattern from the chart and start decreasing on round 23.

Round 23: [K1, ssk, k8, k2tog, k1] x 2 = 24 stitches.

Round 24: [K1, ssk, k6, k2tog, k1] x 2 = 20 stitches.

Round 25: [K1, ssk, k4, k2tog, k1] x 2 = 16 stitches.

Round 26: [K1, ssk, k2, k2tog, k1] x 2 = 12 stitches.

Round 27: [K1, ssk, k2tog, k1] x 2 = 8 stitches.

Close the top of the thumb in the same way as the top of the mitten.

FINISHING

Weave in all ends. Wash and block both mittens, patting them gently to get the right size and to even out the stitches.

Left and right mittens

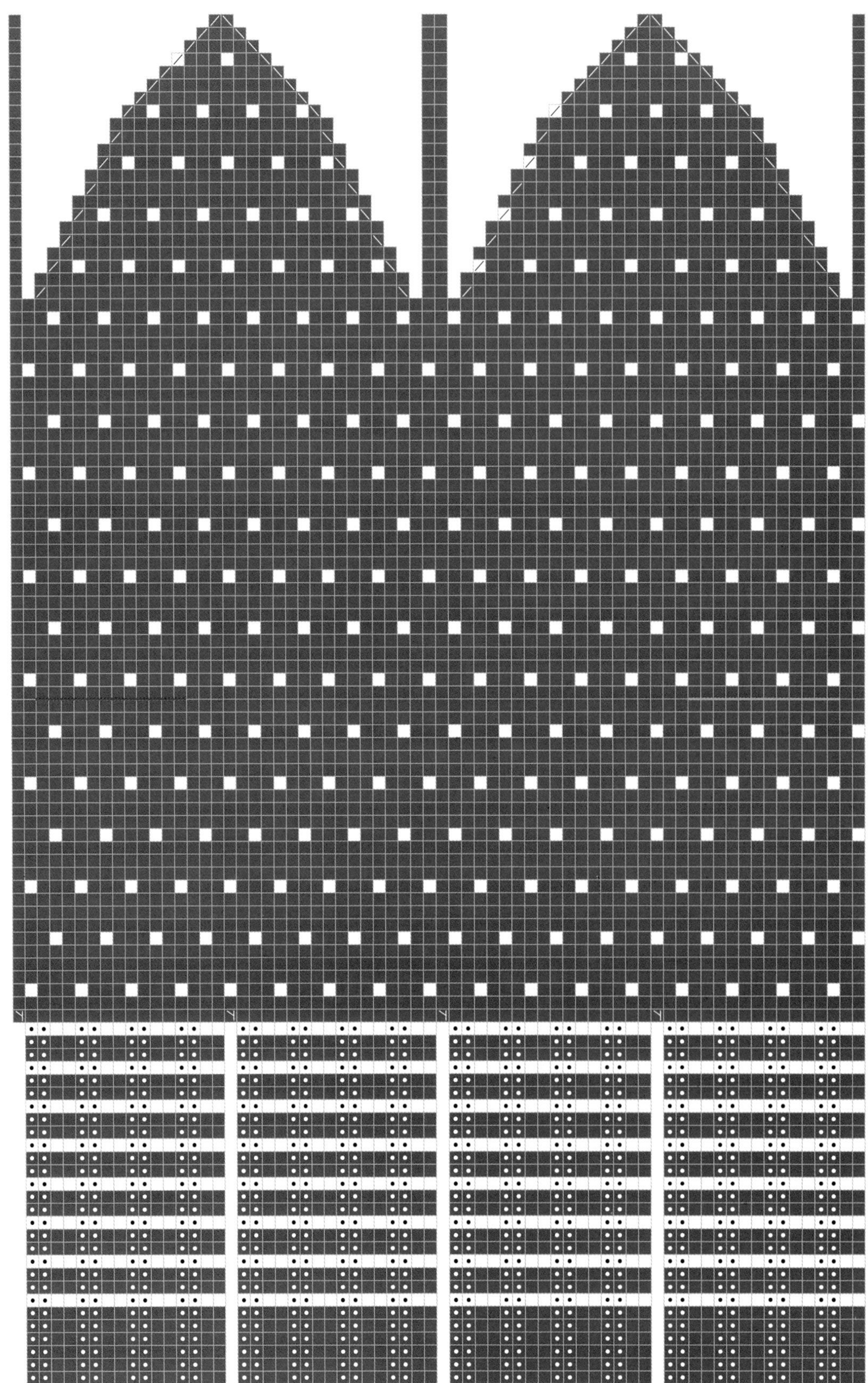

Thumb

Knit—MC **black**
Knit—CC **white**
Purl
M1L
Thumb opening on right mitten
Thumb opening on left mitten
Ssk
K2tog
Pick up and knit stitches on either side of the thumb opening

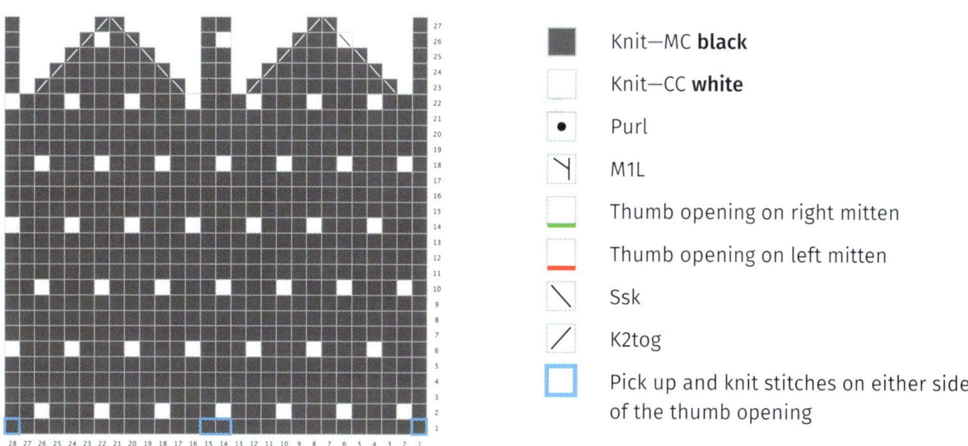

BÁRA

There is something quiet and elegant about these mittens, which were originally entered into a mitten competition held by Halldóra Bjarnadóttir. They probably won or were awarded high marks by Halldóra. The knitter remains unknown. The original mittens are knitted in light brown wool, with dark brown and white used for the contrast colors. The cuff is ribbed, and the thumb is picked up and knitted later in the same pattern as the body of the mitten. This is a deceptively uncomplicated pattern that is a pleasure to knit.

SIZE Women's medium

FINISHED MEASUREMENTS 11.5 in/29 cm long (incl. 2.5 in/6 cm ribbed cuff) and 7 in/18 cm around palm circumference.

YARN CYCA #1 (sock/fingering/baby) *Pirkkalanka Ohut* (100% wool, 437 yd/400 m / 100 g) Main color (MC): brown, 50 g. Contrasting colors (CC): blackish brown, ivory, 25 g of each.

CYCA #1 (sock/fingering/baby) *Rowan Fine Tweed* (100% wool, 98 yd/90 m / 25 g) Main color (MC): burgundy, 50 g. Contrasting colors (CC): curry yellow, lilac, 25 g of each.

Or similar fingering weight wool.

NEEDLES Size US 0/2 mm set of 5 DPNs for the cuff. Size US 1/2.5 mm set of 5 DPNs for the hand. Adjust needle size if necessary to obtain the correct gauge.

OTHER MATERIALS Scrap yarn and tapestry needle.

GAUGE 36 stitches and 36 rounds in stranded color work, on larger needles, after blocking = 4 in/10 cm.

If the gauge is not correct, the mittens might not fit properly.

PATTERN NOTES

- See the section beginning on page 30 for special techniques concerning yarn dominance, decreasing, increasing, and finishing.
- All stitches are knit stitches unless specifically noted otherwise.
- Both mittens are knitted from the same chart.
- Read all chart rounds from right to left.
- The thumb is worked at the beginning of the round on the right mitten and at the end of the round on the left mitten.

CUFF With smaller needles and MC, cast on 62 stitches. Arrange stitches on the needles: 16+16+16+14 stitches and join into round.

Work 22 rounds (2.5 in/6 cm) of ribbing: k1, p1.

HAND

Round 23, inc. round: [K16, M1L] x 3, k14, M1L = 66 stitches.

Change to larger needles and rearrange stitches on the needles: 16+17+16+17 stitches. Work in pattern from the chart to round 53.

Round 53: Work in pattern from the chart while working thumb openings:

RIGHT MITTEN

K2, k12 stitches with scrap yarn (green line on the chart), slip these 12 stitches back onto left needle and knit in pattern to the end of the round.

LEFT MITTEN

Knit until 14 stitches are left in the round. K12 stitches with scrap yarn (red line on the chart), slip these 12 stitches back onto left needle and knit in pattern to the end of the round.

BOTH MITTENS

Work in pattern from the chart to round 93.

START DECREASE ROUNDS

Work in pattern from the chart while working decreases.

Decrease 4 stitches on every round as follows:

Round 93: [K1, ssk, k27, k2tog, k1] x 2 = 62 stitches.

Round 94: [K1, ssk, k25, k2tog, k1] x 2 = 58 stitches.

Round 95: [K1, ssk, k23, k2tog, k1] x 2 = 54 stitches.

Round 96: [K1, ssk, k21, k2tog, k1] x 2 = 50 stitches.

Round 97: [K1, ssk, k19, k2tog, k1] x 2 = 46 stitches.

Round 98: [K1, ssk, k17, k2tog, k1] x 2 = 42 stitches.

Round 99: [K1, ssk, k15, k2tog, k1] x 2 = 38 stitches.

Round 100: [K1, ssk, k13, k2tog, k1] x 2 = 34 stitches.

Round 101: [K1, ssk, k11, k2tog, k1] x 2 = 30 stitches.

Round 102: [K1, ssk, k9, k2tog, k1] x 2 = 26 stitches.

Round 103: [K1, ssk, k7, k2tog, k1] x 2 = 22 stitches.

Round 104: [K1, ssk, k5, k2tog, k1] x 2 = 18 stitches.

Round 105: [K1, ssk, k3, k2tog, k1] x 2 = 14 stitches.

Round 106: [K1, ssk, k1, k2tog, k1] x 2 = 10 stitches.

Close the top of the mitten (see the section about finishing, page 31).

THUMB

Remove scrap yarn, place stitches on 3 needles and knit around in pattern, picking up 2 stitches on either side of the opening and one extra stitch at the top of the opening = 28 stitches. Work in pattern from the chart and start decreasing on round 19.

Round 19: [K1, ssk, k8, k2tog, k1] x 2 = 24 stitches.

Rounds 20 and 22**:** Knit.

Round 21: [K1, ssk, k6, k2tog, k1] x 2 = 20 stitches.

Round 23: [K1, ssk, k4, k2tog, k1] x 2 = 16 stitches.

Round 24: [K1, ssk, k2, k2tog, k1] x 2 = 12 stitches.

Round 25: [K1, ssk, k2tog, k1] x 2 = 8 stitches.

Round 26: [K1, ssk, k1] x 2 = 6 stitches.

Close the top of the thumb in the same way as the top of the mitten.

FINISHING

Weave in all ends. Wash and block both mittens, patting them gently to get the right size and to even out the stitches.

Left and right mittens

Thumb

- Knit—MC **brown**
- Knit—CC **white**
- Knit—CC **blackish brown**
- Purl
- M1L
- K2tog
- Ssk
- Thumb opening on left mitten
- Thumb opening on right mitten
- Pick up and knit stitches on either side of the thumb opening

KRÍA

Very understated mittens from Halldórustofa. They are knitted in light greyish blue wool, which was hand-spun and delicate. It's actually likely that these mittens were mostly machine-knitted, with only the dark blue patterns hand-knit—the blue line of patterning above the cuff and the eight-petal rose on the backs. They are different from other mittens in the book on a technical level, and are suitable for experienced knitters.

SIZE Women's medium

FINISHED MEASUREMENTS 11.5 in/29 cm long (incl. 3 in/8 cm ribbed cuff) and 7 in/18 cm around palm circumference.

YARN CYCA #1 (sock/fingering/baby) *Pirkkalanka Ohut* (100% wool, 437 yd/400 m / 100 g) Main color (MC): light grey, 50 g. Contrasting color (CC): indigo blue, 25 g.

CYCA #1 (sock/fingering/baby) *Rowan Fine Tweed* (100% wool, 98 yd/90 m / 25 g) Main color (MC): dark grey, 50 g. Contrasting color (CC): blue green, 25 g.

Or similar fingering weight wool.

NEEDLES Size US 0/2 mm set of 5 DPNs. Adjust needle size if necessary to obtain the correct gauge.

OTHER MATERIALS Scrap yarn and tapestry needle.

GAUGE 36 stitches and 36 rounds in stockinette stitch, after blocking = 4 in/10 cm.

If the gauge is not correct, the mittens might not fit properly.

PATTERN NOTES

- See the section beginning on page 30 for special techniques concerning yarn dominance, decreasing, increasing, and finishing.
- All stitches are knit stitches unless specifically noted.
- The chart is read from right to left.
- The thumb is worked at the beginning of the round on the right mitten and at the end of the round on the left mitten.
- The eight-petal rose pattern on the back of the hand is knitted with a combination technique of intarsia and stranded colorwork.

CUFF With MC, cast on 66 stitches using the long-tail cast on (see the section about cast-ons, page 28, for other methods). Arrange stitches on the needles: 16+16+16+18 stitches and join into round.

Work 29 rounds (3 in/8 cm) of ribbing: K1, p1.

HAND

Work in pattern from the chart to round 48.

Round 48: Work the thumb openings as follows:

RIGHT MITTEN

K1, k11 stitches with scrap yarn (green line on the chart), slip these 11 stitches back onto left needle and knit in pattern to the end of the round.

LEFT MITTEN

Knit until 12 stitches are left in the round. K11 stitches with scrap yarn (red line on the chart), slip these 11 stitches back onto left needle and knit in pattern to the end of the round.

Rounds 49–74:

Knit with MC until you reach the pattern. Work the pattern from the chart with CC. After working the first row of the pattern, leave the CC yarn (on the left side of the pattern) and pick up the MC strand (on the right side of the pattern) and twist it around the CC strand and knit the round until you reach the rose again in round 2 of the pattern. The CC yarn will be on the other (wrong) side of the pattern. Take the CC strand and lay it across the back of the rose pattern, taking care not to stretch the float too much, twist the CC and MC strands (to prevent making a hole) and knit the second round of the rose pattern. *At the same time*, catch the back yarn every few stitches to shorten the floats. This part of the mitten will be thicker than the rest. Repeat this throughout the pattern.

After the eight-petal pattern has been knit, carry on working from the chart until the decreases at the top of the mitten have been reached, round 88, or when the top of the little finger has been reached.

START DECREASE ROUNDS

RIGHT MITTEN

Round 88: K1, ssk, k26, k2tog, k2, ssk, k28, k2tog, k1 = 62 stitches.

Rounds 89, 91, 93, 95, 97, and 99: Knit.

Round 90: K1, ssk, k24, k2tog, k2, ssk, k26, k2tog, k1 = 58 stitches.

Round 92: K1, ssk, k22, k2tog, k2, ssk, k24, k2tog, k1 = 54 stitches.

Round 94: K1, ssk, k20, k2tog, k2, ssk, k22, k2tog, k1 = 50 stitches.

Round 96: K1, ssk, k18, k2tog, k2, ssk, k20, k2tog, k1 = 46 stitches.

Round 98: K1, ssk, k16, k2tog, k2, ssk, k18, k2tog, k1 = 42 stitches.

Round 100: K1, ssk, k14, k2tog, k2, ssk, k16, k2tog, k1 = 38 stitches.

Round 101: K19, ssk, k14, k2tog, k1 = 36 stitches.

LEFT MITTEN

Round 88: K1, ssk, k28, k2tog, k2, ssk, k26, k2tog, k1 = 62 stitches.

Rounds 89, 91, 93, 95, 97, and 99: Knit.

Round 90: K1, ssk, k26, k2tog, k2, ssk, k24, k2tog, k1 = 58 stitches.

Round 92: K1, ssk, k24, k2tog, k2, ssk, k22, k2tog, k1 = 54 stitches.

Round 94: K1, ssk, k22, k2tog, k2, ssk, k20, k2tog, k1 = 50 stitches.

Round 96: K1, ssk, k20, k2tog, k2, ssk, k18, k2tog, k1 = 46 stitches.

Round 98: K1, ssk, k18, k2tog, k2, ssk, k16, k2tog, k1 = 42 stitches.

Round 100: K1, ssk, k16, k2tog, k2, ssk, k14, k2tog, k1 = 38 stitches.

Round 101: K1, ssk, k14, k2tog, k19 = 36 stitches.

BOTH MITTENS

Round 102: [K1, ssk, k12, k2tog, k1] x 2 = 32 stitches.

Round 103: [K1, ssk, k10, k2tog, k1] x 2 = 28 stitches.

Round 104: [K1, ssk, k8, k2tog, k1] x 2 = 24 stitches.

Round 105: [K1, ssk, k6, k2tog, k1] x 2 = 20 stitches.

Round 106: [K1, ssk, k4, k2tog, k1] x 2 = 16 stitches.

Round 107: [K1, ssk, k2, k2tog, k1] x 2 = 12 stitches.

Round 108: [K1, ssk, k2tog, k1] x 2 = 8 stitches.

Close the top of the mitten (see the section about finishing, page 31).

THUMB

Remove scrap yarn, place stitches on 3 needles and knit around, picking up 2 stitches on either side of the opening = 26 stitches. Knit with MC and start decreasing on round 22.

Round 22: [Ssk, k8, k2tog, k1] x 2 = 22 stitches.

Round 23: [Ssk, k6, k2tog, k1] x 2 = 18 stitches.

Round 24: [Ssk, k4, k2tog, k1] x 2 = 14 stitches.

Round 25: [Ssk, k2, k2tog, k1] x 2 = 10 stitches.

Round 26: [Ssk, k2tog, k1] x 2 = 6 stitches.

Close the top of the thumb in the same way as the top of the mitten.

FINISHING

Weave in all ends. Wash and block both mittens, patting them gently to get the right size and to even out the stitches.

Left mitten

Thumb

Knit—MC **light grey**
Knit—CC **indigo blue**
Purl
K2tog
Ssk
Thumb opening on right mitten
Thumb opening on left mitten
Pick up and knit stitches on either side of the thumb opening

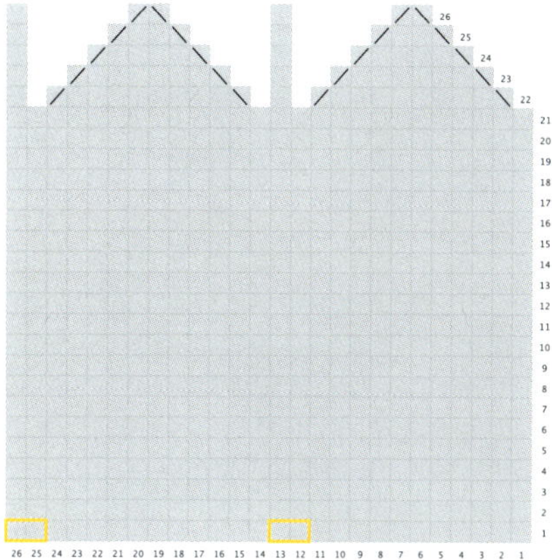

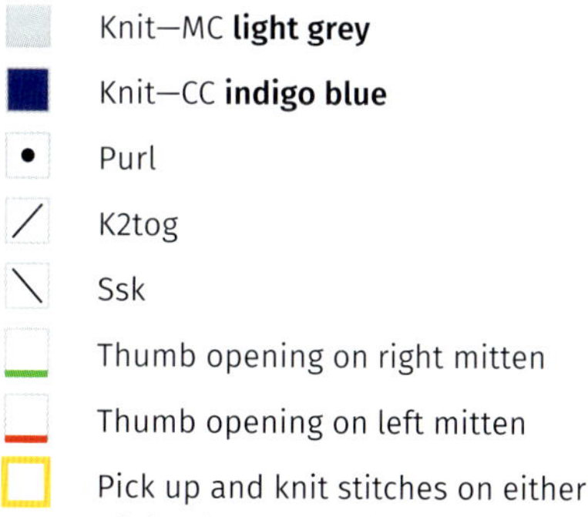

SAGA

These mittens from Halldórustofa are knitted in hand-spun dark brown with a white contrasting wool. The cuffs are knitted with one stitch in white and one in brown alternately for one round and then the pattern is shifted in the next round. This makes the cuff very dense. The original mittens show signs of wear and have been mended. The mitten body and the thumb are patterned throughout. It's important to keep an even tension and work the dominant color consistently.

SIZE Women's medium

FINISHED MEASUREMENTS 11 in/27.5 cm long (incl. 3 in/7.5 cm cuff) and 7 in/18 cm around palm circumference.

YARN CYCA #1 (sock/fingering/baby) *Pirkkalanka Ohut* (100% wool, 437 yd/400 m / 100 g) Main color (MC): dark brown, 50 g. Contrasting color (CC): white, 50 g.

CYCA #1 (sock/fingering/baby) *Rowan Fine Tweed* (100% wool, 98 yd/90 m / 25 g) Main color (MC): green, 50 g. Contrasting color (CC): dark blue, 50 g.

Or similar fingering weight wool.

NEEDLES Size US 0/2 mm set of 5 DPNs for the cuff. Size US 1/2.5 mm set of 5 DPNs for the hand. Adjust needle size if necessary to obtain the correct gauge.

OTHER MATERIALS Scrap yarn and tapestry needle.

GAUGE 38 stitches and 36 rounds in stranded colorwork, on larger needles, after blocking = 4 in/10 cm.

If the gauge is not correct, the mittens might not fit properly.

PATTERN NOTES

- See the section beginning on page 30 for special techniques concerning yarn dominance, decreasing, increasing, and finishing.
- All stitches are knit stitches unless specifically noted otherwise.
- Both mittens are knitted from the same chart.
- Read all chart rounds from right to left.
- The thumb is worked at the beginning of the round on the right mitten and at the end of the round on the left mitten.

CUFF With smaller needles and MC, cast on 60 stitches. Arrange evenly on the needles and join into round. Purl the first two rounds and then follow the chart for the cuff to round 29.

HAND

Round 29, inc. round: [K10, M1L] x 6 = 66 stitches.

Change to larger needles. Arrange stitches on the needles: 16+17+16+17. Work in pattern from the chart to round 49.

Round 49: Work in pattern from the chart while working thumb openings:

RIGHT MITTEN

K2, k13 stitches with scrap yarn (yellow line on the chart), slip these 13 stitches back onto left needle and knit in pattern to the end of the round.

LEFT MITTEN

Knit until 15 stitches are left in the round. K13 stitches with scrap yarn (red line on the chart), slip these 13 stitches back onto left needle and knit in pattern to the end of the round.

BOTH MITTENS

Work in pattern from the chart to round 90.

START DECREASE ROUNDS

Work in pattern from the chart while working decreases.
Decrease 4 stitches on every round as follows:

Round 90: [K1, ssk, k27, k2tog, k1] x 2 = 62 stitches.

Round 91: [K1, ssk, k25, k2tog, k1] x 2 = 58 stitches.

Round 92: [K1, ssk, k23, k2tog, k1] x 2 = 54 stitches.

Round 93: [K1, ssk, k21, k2tog, k1] x 2 = 50 stitches.

Round 94: [K1, ssk, k19, k2tog, k1] x 2 = 46 stitches.

Round 95: [K1, ssk, k17, k2tog, k1] x 2 = 42 stitches.

Round 96: [K1, ssk, k15, k2tog, k1] x 2 = 38 stitches.

Round 97: [K1, ssk, k13, k2tog, k1] x 2 = 34 stitches.

Round 98: [K1, ssk, k11, k2tog, k1] x 2 = 30 stitches.

Round 99: [K1, ssk, k9, k2tog, k1] x 2 = 26 stitches.

Round 100: [K1, ssk, k7, k2tog, k1] x 2 = 22 stitches.

Round 101: [K1, ssk, k5, k2tog, k1] x 2 = 18 stitches.

Round 102: [K1, ssk, k3, k2tog, k1] x 2 = 14 stitches.

Round 103: [K1, ssk, k1, k2tog, k1] x 2 = 10 stitches.

Close the top of the mitten (see the section about finishing, page 31).

THUMB

Remove scrap yarn, place stitches on 3 needles and knit around in pattern, picking up 2 stitches on either side of the opening and one extra stitch at the top of the opening = 30 stitches. Work in pattern from the chart and start decreasing on round 21.

Round 21: [K1, ssk, k9, k2tog, k1] x 2 = 26 stitches.

Round 22: [K1, ssk, k7, k2tog, k1] x 2 = 22 stitches.

Round 23: [K1, ssk, k5, k2tog, k1] x 2 = 18 stitches.

Round 24: [K1, ssk, k3, k2tog, k1] x 2 = 14 stitches.

Round 25: [K1, ssk, k1, k2tog, k1] x 2 = 10 stitches.

Round 26: [K1, sl1, k2tog, psso, k1] x 2 = 6 stitches.

Close the top of the thumb in the same way as the top of the mitten.

FINISHING

Weave in all ends. Wash and block both mittens, patting them gently to get the right size and to even out the stitches.

Left and right mittens

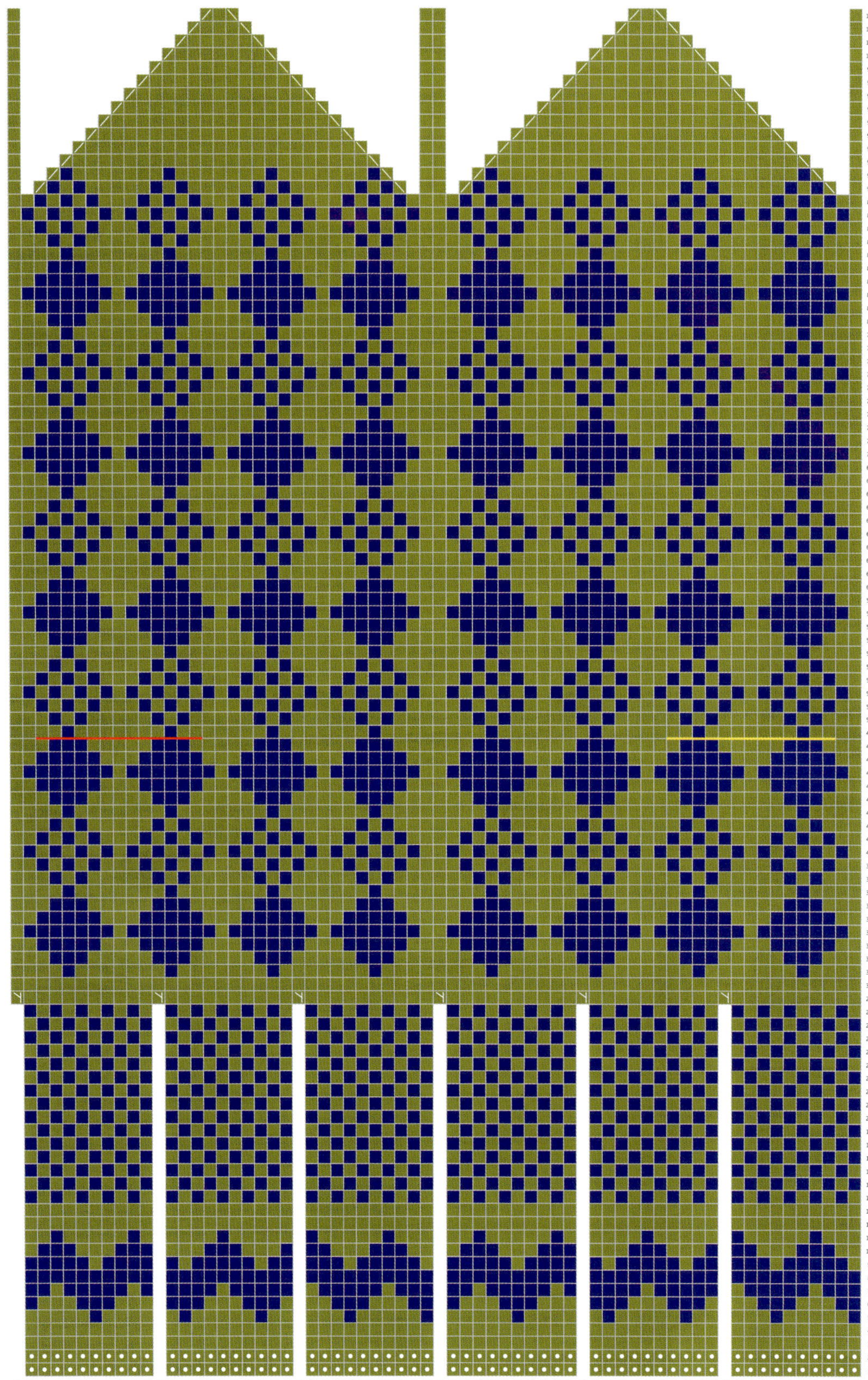

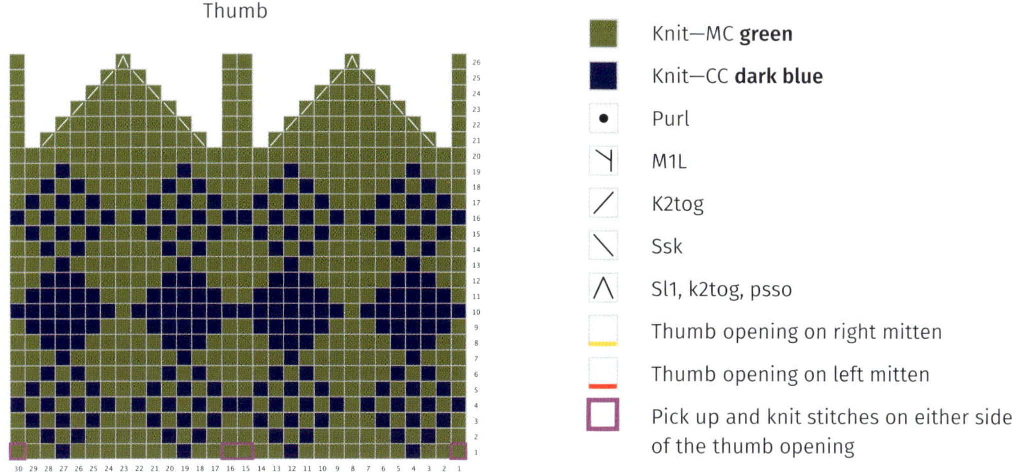
Thumb
Knit—MC **green**
Knit—CC **dark blue**
Purl
M1L
K2tog
Ssk
Sl1, k2tog, psso
Thumb opening on right mitten
Thumb opening on left mitten
Pick up and knit stitches on either side of the thumb opening

SÓLEY

These beautiful gloves were knitted by Signý Benediktsdóttir (1900–1991) from Balaskarð. She worked in the initials FG—presumably those of the recipient, a man named Finnur Guðmundsson from Skrapatunga. He died in 1971, so the gloves are at least 50 years old. These gloves are knitted with black as the main color and white as the contrast color. It's always a challenge to knit gloves, especially when they are worked with stranded knitting. A project for an experienced knitter—and, of course, you can knit your own initials into the project.

SIZE Women's medium

FINISHED MEASUREMENTS 11.5 in/29 cm long to end of middle finger (incl. 2.5 in/8.0 cm ribbed cuff) and 7.5 in/19 cm around palm circumference.

YARN CYCA #1 (sock/fingering/baby) *Pirkkalanka Ohut* (100% wool, 437 yd/400 m / 100 g) Main color (MC): black, 50 g. Contrasting color (CC): white, 50 g.

CYCA #1 (sock/fingering/baby) *Rowan Fine Tweed* (100% wool, 98 yd/90 m / 25 g) Main color (MC): dark red, 50 g. Contrasting color (CC): dark blue, 50 g.

Or similar fingering weight wool.

NEEDLES Size US 0/2 mm set of 5 DPNs for the cuff. Size US 1/2.5 mm set of 5 DPNs for the hand. Adjust needle size if necessary to obtain the correct gauge.

OTHER MATERIALS Scrap yarn and tapestry needle.

GAUGE 37 stitches and 38 rounds in stranded colorwork, on larger needles, after blocking = 4 in/10 cm.

If the gauge is not correct, the gloves might not fit properly.

PATTERN NOTES

- See the section beginning on page 30 for special techniques concerning yarn dominance, decreasing, increasing, and finishing.
- The cuff is knit in 2 x 2 rib and the body and the thumb follow the chart.
- Read the chart from right to left for both gloves; on the right glove, the palm is knitted first, and then the back. On the left glove, the back is knitted first, followed by the palm.
- These gloves have a thumb gusset. The beginning of the gusset is marked with a pink line.
- The chart for the fingers shows only the fingers on the right glove. For the left glove, make sure the checked pattern matches up on the palm side of the glove and continue to knit the checked pattern as established.

- To make the knitter's initials for this pattern, an alphabet is shown here below. The letters are all of equal height in stitches but of different widths, as they can be 4-12 squares wide. Most letters are 7–9 squares wide. If there isn't enough space, one letter can be placed in the center or the diamonds skipped on either side. Choose your letters and center them instead of the ones on the chart.

RIGHT GLOVE

CUFF

With smaller needles and MC, cast on 60 stitches. Arrange stitches on the needles: 12+16+16+16 stitches and join into round.

Work the cuff in k2, p2 rib: 10 rounds MC, 2 rounds CC, 4 rounds MC, 2 rounds CC, 4 rounds MC, 2 rounds CC and 7 rounds MC. 31 rounds in total.

HAND

Change to larger needles. Work the following 7 rounds in MC.**

Round 32, inc. round: [K9, kfb] x 6 = 66 stitches.

Arrange stitches on 4 needles: 10+19+19+18 stitches.

Rounds 33–34: Knit.

Increases for the thumb begin on the next round.

Round 35: M1R, k1, M1L, k65 = 68 stitches.

Rounds 36–37: Knit.

Round 38: M1R, k3, M1L, k65 = 70 stitches.

Begin stranded colorwork from the chart. Choose what letters are to be used in the chart and center them on the back of the glove.

Rounds 39–40: Knit.

Round 41: M1R, k5, M1L, k65 = 72 stitches.

Rounds 42–43: Knit.

Round 44: M1R, k7, M1L, k65 = 74 stitches.

Rounds 45–46: Knit.

Round 47: M1R, k9, M1L, k65 = 76 stitches.

Rounds 48–49: Knit.

Round 50: M1R, k11, M1L, k65 = 78 stitches.

Rounds 51–52: Knit.

Round 53: Place the 13 thumb gusset stitches on scrap yarn. Cast on 10 stitches in their place following the chart = 75 stitches.

Follow the chart until 80 rounds are completed.

FINGERS

Each finger is now worked separately. Follow the chart and make sure the checked pattern matches up on the palm side of the glove. Stitches from the back and the palm are knitted along with the stitches that are cast on or picked up between each of the fingers.

INDEX FINGER

Place the first 10 stitches of the round on one needle and the last 10 stitches of the round on another needle. Place all the other glove stitches on scrap yarn while this finger is worked. Cast on 4 stitches between the index and middle fingers = 24 stitches. Even the stitches out over 3 needles. The round begins in the center of the 4 cast-on stitches between index and middle fingers.

Knit 24 rounds from the chart.

DECREASE

Round 25: [Ssk, k8, k2tog] x 2 = 20 stitches.

Round 26: Knit.

Round 27: [Ssk, k6, k2tog] x 2 = 16 stitches.

Round 28: Knit.

Round 29: [Ssk, k4, k2tog] x 2 = 12 stitches.

Round 30: [Ssk, k2, k2tog] x 2 = 8 stitches.

Round 31: [Ssk, k2tog] x 2 = 4 stitches.

Close the top of the finger (see the section about finishing, page 31).

MIDDLE FINGER

Place the next 10 stitches of the palm on one needle and the next 9 stitches of the back on another needle. Pick up and knit 3 stitches between the middle finger and the index finger and cast on 2 stitches between the middle finger and the ring finger = 24 stitches. Even the stitches out over 3 needles. The round begins with the last picked up stitch before the palm, between index and middle fingers.

Knit 26 rounds from the chart.

DECREASE

Round 27: [Ssk, k8, k2tog] x 2 = 20 stitches.

Round 28: Knit.

Round 29: [Ssk, k6, k2tog] x 2 = 16 stitches.

Round 30: Knit.

Round 31: [Ssk, k4, k2tog] x 2 = 12 stitches.

Round 32: [Ssk, k2, k2tog] x 2 = 8 stitches.

Round 33: [Ssk, k2tog] x 2 = 4 stitches.

Close the top of the finger as before.

RING FINGER

Place the next 9 stitches of the palm on one needle and the next 9 stitches of the back on another needle. Pick up and knit 3 stitches between the ring finger and the middle finger and cast on 3 stitches between the ring finger and the little finger = 24 stitches. Even the stitches out over 3 needles. The round begins with the last picked up stitch before the palm, between middle and ring fingers.

Knit 24 rounds from the chart.

DECREASE

Round 25: [Ssk, k8, k2tog] x 2 = 20 stitches.

Round 26: Knit.

Round 27: [Ssk, k6, k2tog] x 2 = 16 stitches.

Round 28: Knit.

Round 29: [Ssk, k4, k2tog] x 2 = 12 stitches.

Round 30: [Ssk, k2, k2tog] x 2 = 8 stitches.

Round 31: [Ssk, k2tog] x 2 = 4 stitches.

Close the top of the finger as before.

LITTLE FINGER

Place the last 9 stitches of the palm on one needle and the last 9 stitches of the back on another needle. Pick up and knit 4 stitches between the little finger and the ring finger = 22 stitches. Even the stitches out over 3 needles. The round begins in the center of the 4 cast on stitches between ring and little fingers.

Knit 18 rounds from the chart.

DECREASE

Round 19: [Ssk, k7, k2tog] x 2 = 18 stitches.

Round 20: Knit.

Round 21: [Ssk, k5, k2tog] x 2 = 14 stitches.

Round 22: Knit.

Round 23: [Ssk, k3, k2tog] x 2 = 10 stitches.

Round 24: [Ssk, k1, k2tog] x 2 = 6 stitches.

Close the top of the finger as before.

THUMB

Divide the 13 stitches held on the scrap yarn on two needles. Pick up and knit 10 stitches at the back of the thumb using appropriate pattern color and the third needle and pick up and knit 2 stitches at either side = 27 stitches.

Knit 23 rounds from the chart.

DECREASE

Round 25: Ssk, k9, k2tog, ssk, k10, k2tog = 23 stitches.

Round 26: Ssk, k7, k2tog, ssk, k8, k2tog = 19 stitches.

Round 27: Ssk, k5, k2tog, ssk, k6, k2tog = 15 stitches.

Round 28: Ssk, k3, k2tog, ssk, k4, k2tog = 11 stitches.

Round 29: Ssk, k1, k2tog, ssk, k2, k2tog = 7 stitches.

Close the top of the thumb as other fingers.

LEFT GLOVE

Work the left glove like the right until **.

Increases for the thumb gusset are the same as on the right glove except the gusset is at the end of the round.

Round 32: [Kfb, k9] x 6 = 66 stitches.

Arrange stitches on 4 needles: 18+19+19+10 stitches.

Round 33–34: Knit.

Round 35: K65, M1R, k1, M1L = 68 stitches.

Rounds 36–37: Knit.

Round 38: K65, M1R, k3, M1L = 70 stitches.

Begin stranded colorwork from the chart. Choose what letters are to be used in the chart and center them on the back of the glove.

Rounds 39–40: Knit.

Round 41: K65, M1R, k5, M1L = 72 stitches.

Rounds 42–43: Knit.

Round 44: K65, M1R, k7, M1L = 74 stitches.

Rounds 45–46: Knit.

Round 47: K65, M1R, k9, M1L = 76 stitches.

Rounds 48–49: Knit.

Round 50: K65, M1R, k11, M1L = 78 stitches.

Rounds 51–52: Knit.

Round 53: Knit from the chart until 13 stitches remain. Place these 13 thumb gusset stitches on scrap yarn and cast on 10 stitches in their place.

Follow the chart until 80 rounds are completed.

FINGERS

Each finger is now worked separately. Follow the directions for the right glove except that the little finger is knitted first, then the ring finger, the middle finger, and lastly the index finger. (There is a separate chart for the left thumb.) For each finger of the left hand, make sure the checked pattern matches up on the palm side of the glove and continue to knit the checked pattern as established.

FINISHING

Weave in all ends. Wash and block both gloves, patting them gently to get the right size and to even out the stitches.

Left glove

Right glove

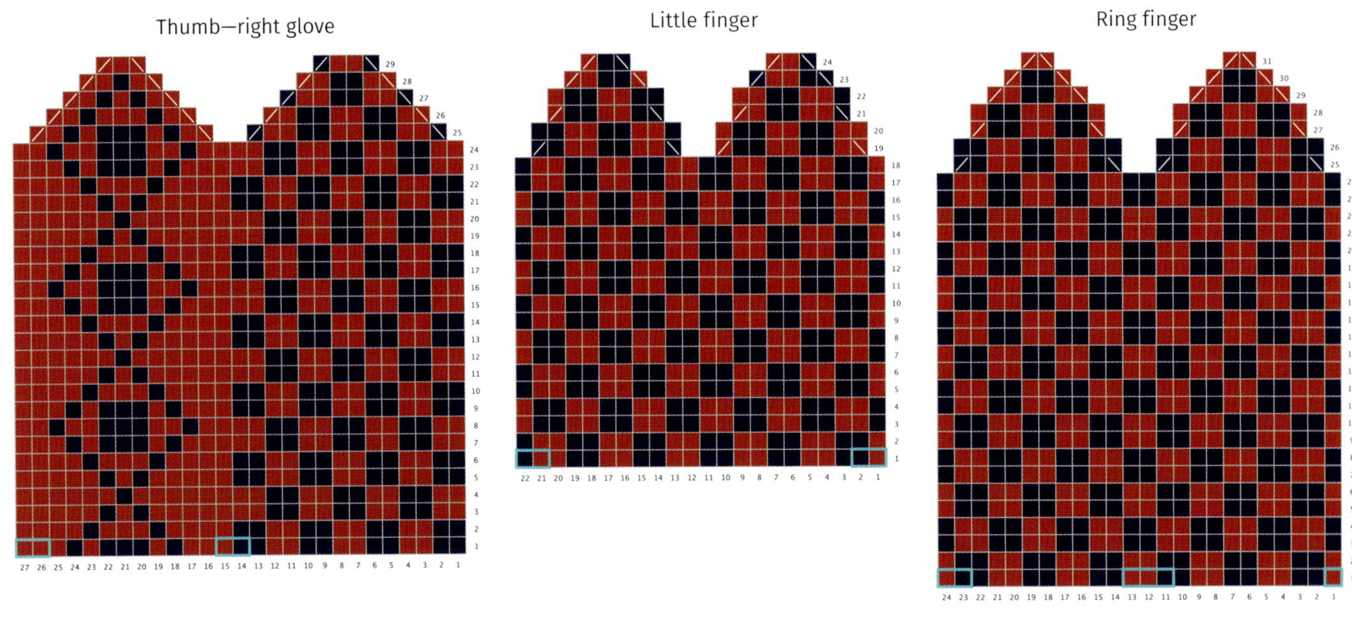
Thumb—right glove
Little finger
Ring finger

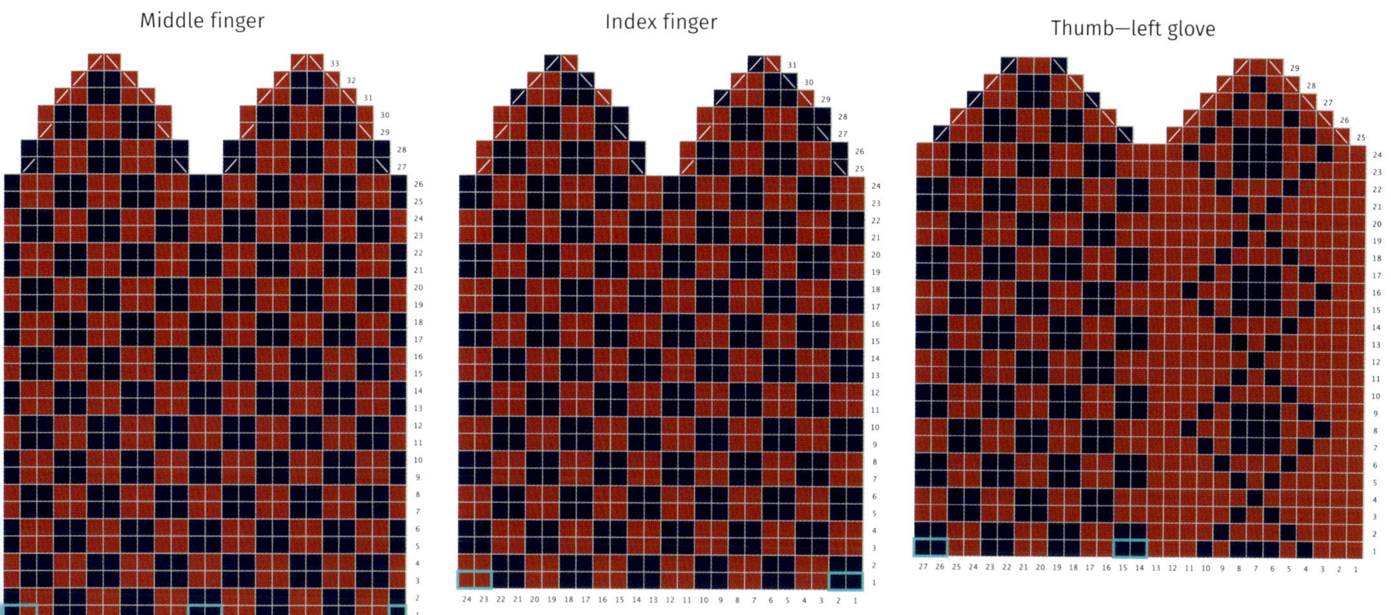
Middle finger
Index finger
Thumb—left glove

Knit—MC **dark red**
Knit—CC **dark blue**
Purl
Kfb
K2tog
Ssk
M1R
M1L
Start thumb gusset
Thumb opening
Thumb opening on right mitten
Outlines of fingers —knit from the finger charts

SUNNA

These classic, neatly patterned mittens are preserved in the Textile Museum. They were entered into a knitting competition held by Halldóra Bjarnadóttir; the knitter is unknown. The originals are knitted with a yellow contrasting color on a black main color. The combination is unusual for the museum's collection, which predominantly consists of mittens made with undyed wool. The pattern is reminiscent of machine-knitted pullovers from the middle of the 20th century. This design is perfect for beginners.

SIZE — Women's medium

FINISHED MEASUREMENTS — 11 in/27 cm long (incl. 2 in/5 cm ribbed cuff) and 7.5 in/18 cm around palm circumference.

YARN — CYCA #1 (sock/fingering/baby) *Rowan Fine Tweed* (100% wool, 98 yd/90 m / 25 g)
Main color (MC): black, 50 g. Contrasting color (CC): curry yellow, 50 g.

Or CYCA #2 (sport/baby) *Mohair by Canard Kid Mohair 2-ply* (65% Mohair, 35% Merino, 193 yd/176 m / 50 g)
Main color (MC): dark grey, 50 g. Contrasting color (CC): green, 50 g.

Or similar fingering weight wool.

NEEDLES — Size US 0/2 mm set of 5 DPNs for the cuff. Size US 1/2.5 mm set of 5 DPNs for the hand. Adjust needle size if necessary to obtain the correct gauge.

OTHER MATERIALS — Scrap yarn and tapestry needle.

GAUGE — 36 stitches and 36 rounds in stranded colorwork, on larger needles, after blocking = 4 in/10 cm.

If the gauge is not correct, the mittens might not fit properly.

PATTERN NOTES

- See the section beginning on page 30 for special techniques concerning yarn dominance, decreasing, increasing, and finishing.
- All stitches are knit stitches unless specifically noted otherwise.
- Both mittens are knitted from the same chart.
- Read all chart rounds from right to left.
- The thumb is worked at the beginning of the round on the right mitten and at the end of the round on the left mitten.

CUFF — With smaller needles and MC, cast on 60 stitches. Arrange evenly on the needles and join into round. Work 24 rounds (2 in/5 cm) of ribbing: k2, p1.

HAND

Change to larger needles.

Round 25, inc. round: [K6, kfb, k7, kfb] x 4 = 68 stitches.

Work in pattern from the chart to round 55.

Round 55: Work in pattern from the chart while working thumb openings:

RIGHT MITTEN

K2, k12 stitches with scrap yarn (green line on the chart), slip these 12 stitches back onto left needle and knit in pattern to the end of the round.

LEFT MITTEN

Knit until 14 stitches are left in the round. K12 stitches with scrap yarn (red line on the chart), slip these 12 stitches back onto left needle and knit in pattern to the end of the round.

BOTH MITTENS

Work in pattern from chart to round 89.

START DECREASE ROUNDS

Work in pattern from the chart while working decreases.
Decrease 4 stitches on the indicated rounds as follows:

Round 89: [Ssk, k30, k2tog] x 2 = 64 stitches.

Rounds 90, 92, 94, 96, 98, 100, and 102: Knit.

Round 91: [Ssk, k28, k2tog] x 2 = 60 stitches.

Round 93: [Ssk, k26, k2tog] x 2 = 56 stitches.

Round 95: [Ssk, k24, k2tog] x 2 = 52 stitches.

Round 97: [Ssk, k22, k2tog] x 2 = 48 stitches.

Round 99: [Ssk, k20, k2tog] x 2 = 44 stitches.

Round 101: [Ssk, k18, k2tog] x 2 = 40 stitches.

Round 103: [Ssk, k16, k2tog] x 2 = 36 stitches

Round 104: [Ssk, k14, k2tog] x 2 = 32 stitches.

Round 105: [Ssk, k12, k2tog] x 2 = 28 stitches.

Round 106: [Ssk, k10, k2tog] x 2 = 24 stitches.

Round 107: [Ssk, k8, k2tog] x 2 = 20 stitches.

Round 108: [Ssk, k6, k2tog] x 2 = 16 stitches.

Round 109: [Ssk, k4, k2tog] x 2 = 12 stitches.

Round 110: [Ssk, k2, k2tog] x 2 = 8 stitches.

Close the top of the mitten (see the section about finishing, page 31).

THUMB

Remove scrap yarn, place stitches on 3 needles and knit around in pattern, picking up 2 stitches on either side of the opening and one extra stitch at the top of the opening = 28 stitches. Work in pattern from the chart and start decreasing on round 23.

Round 23: [Ssk, k10, k2tog] x 2 = 24 stitches.

Round 24: [Ssk, k8, k2tog] x 2 = 20 stitches.

Round 25: [Ssk, k6, k2tog] x 2 = 16 stitches.

Round 26: [Ssk, k4, k2tog] x 2 = 12 stitches.

Round 27: [Ssk, k2, k2tog] x 2 = 8 stitches.

Round 28: [Ssk, k2tog] x 2 = 4 stitches.

Close the top of the thumb in the same way as the top of the mitten.

FINISHING

Weave in all ends. Wash and block both mittens, patting them gently to get the right size and to even out the stitches.

Left and right mittens

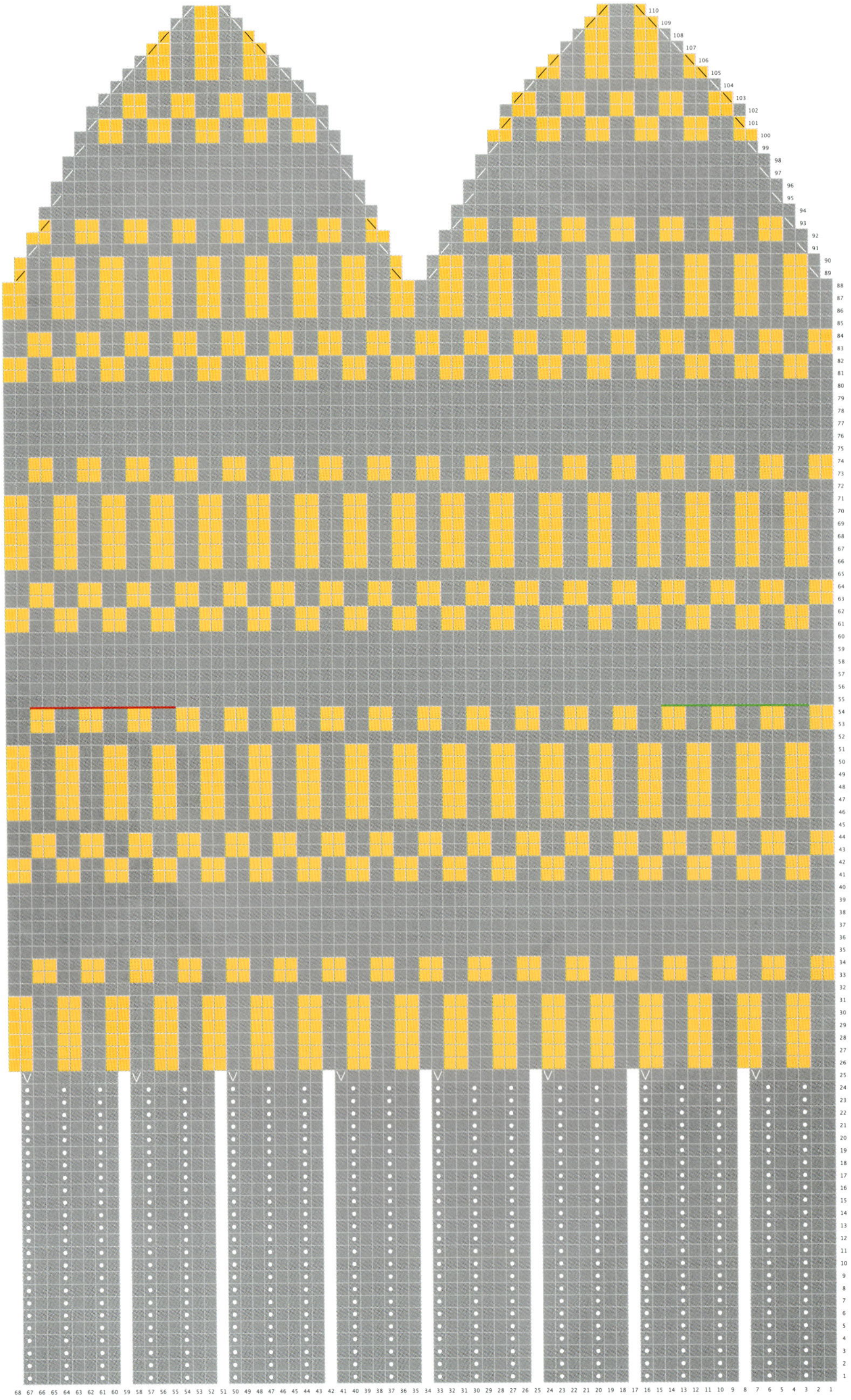

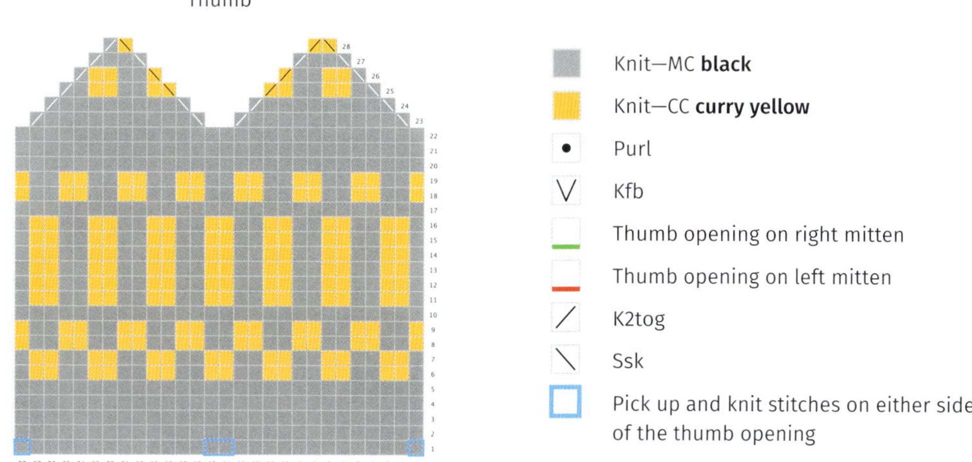
Thumb
Knit—MC **black**
Knit—CC **curry yellow**
Purl
Kfb
Thumb opening on right mitten
Thumb opening on left mitten
K2tog
Ssk
Pick up and knit stitches on either side of the thumb opening

RÚNA

These mittens for special occasions were originally knit with a very fine, silky yarn. They are very different from other mittens in the Textile Museum. Guðrún Jónsdóttir (1916–2014) from Hnjúkur knitted and donated these mittens to the collection. The thumb gusset is knitted on the side, the palms are stockinette stitch, and the backs are a peacock stitch. The bottom hem is a turned picot edge. These mittens can be knit in a variety of yarns. The peacock pattern is fun to knit for the experienced knitter. There are two yarn options for these mittens—silk or mohair. Choose one type of yarn and use it throughout the pattern.

SIZE
Women's medium

The pattern on the back of the mittens is quite stretchy with a lot of give, so the fit should be fairly tight.

These mittens fit a medium women's size even though the gauges are very different for the two types of yarn used.

FINISHED MEASUREMENTS
Silk version: 11 in/28 cm long and 6 in/15 cm around palm circumference.

Mohair version: 10.5 in/26.5 cm long and 7 in/17 cm palm circumference.

YARN
CYCA #1 (sock/fingering/baby) *Silkindian Fine Duke 1-ply silk* (100% silk, 400 yd/336 m / 100 g)
Red, 50 g.

OR CYCA #2 (sport/baby) *Mohair by Canard Kid Mohair 2-ply* (65% Mohair, 35% Merino, 193 yd/176 m / 50 g)
Silver grey, 100 g.

Or similar fingering weight yarn.

NEEDLES
Size US 0/2 mm set of 5 DPNs. Adjust needle size if necessary to obtain the correct gauge.

OTHER MATERIALS
2 stitch markers, scrap yarn, and tapestry needle.

GAUGE
Silk version: 38 stitches and 40 rounds in stocking stitch, after blocking = 4 in/10 cm.

Mohair version: 34 stitches and 44 rounds in stocking stitch, after blocking = 4 in/10 cm.

If the gauge is not correct, the mittens might not fit properly.

PATTERN NOTES
- See the section beginning on page 30 for special techniques concerning yarn dominance, decreasing, increasing, and finishing.
- All stitches are knit stitches unless specifically noted otherwise.
- The chart is read from right to left.
- The mittens have a thumb gusset and gusset behind the thumb, which ends on round 69 (marked with a purple line).
- The mittens have a sewn hem with a picot edge.
- The top of the mitten can either be grafted or bound off on the WS.

PEACOCK'S TAIL PATTERN ON THE BACK

The first round is increased by 12 stitches, which are gradually decreased over the following rounds. After 7 rounds, the stitch count is the same as at the beginning.

One pattern repeat: 31 stitches and 7 rounds

Round 1: P1, k9, [yo, k1] x 11, yo, k9, p1 = 43 stitches.

Round 2: P1, k6, k2tog, k25, ssk, k6, p1 = 41 stitches.

Round 3: P1, k5, k2tog, k25, ssk, k5, p1 = 39 stitches.

Round 4: P1, k4, k2tog, k25, ssk, k4, p1 = 37 stitches.

Round 5: P1, k3, k2tog, k25, ssk, k3, p1 = 35 stitches.

Round 6: P1, k2, k2tog, k25, ssk, k2, p1 = 33 stitches.

Round 7: P1, k1, k2tog, k25, ssk, k1, p1 = 31 stitches.

The pattern is worked the same on the back of both mittens and begins in the 11th round. It is worked 12 times in total before the decreases at the top of the mittens. The thumb gusset starts on the 31st round (marked yellow on the chart) and all palm stitches are knitted in stocking stitch.

CUFF

Cast on 60 stitches. Arrange stitches on 3 or 4 needles and join into round. It can be easier to work with all the back stitches on the same needle.

Rounds 1–4: Knit.

RIGHT MITTEN

Round 5, picot round: *K2tog, yo*. Repeat from * to * to end of round.

Rounds 6–10: [K29, p1] x 2.

Rounds 11–17: K29, work the Peacock's Tail pattern.

Rounds 18–24: Repeat rounds 11–17.

Round 25: K29, work pattern round 1 = 72 stitches.

Round 26: K29, work pattern round 2 = 70 stitches.

Round 27: K29, work pattern round 3 = 68 stitches.

Round 28: K29, work pattern round 4 = 66 stitches.

Round 29: K29, work pattern round 5 = 64 stitches.

Round 30: K29, work pattern round 6 = 62 stitches.

THUMB GUSSET

Right thumb increases begin on the 31st round. Place a marker on either side of the increases. The markers are moved between the needles when they are encountered. Always increase on the left side of the first marker and the right side of the second marker.

Round 31: K3, pm, M1R, k1, M1L, pm, k25, work pattern round 7 = 62 stitches.

Round 32: K3, sm, k3, sm, k25, work pattern round 1 = 74 stitches.

Round 33: K3, sm, k3, sm, k25, work pattern round 2 = 72 stitches.

Round 34: K3, sm, M1R, k3, M1L, sm, k25, work pattern round 3 = 72 stitches.

Round 35: K3, sm, k5, sm, k25, work pattern round 4 = 70 stitches.

Round 36: K3, sm, k5, sm, k25, work pattern round 5 = 68 stitches.

Round 37: K3, sm, M1R, k5, M1L, sm, k25, work pattern round 6 = 68 stitches.

Round 38: K3, sm, k7, sm, k25, work pattern round 7 = 66 stitches.

Round 39: K3, sm, k7, sm, k25, work pattern round 1 = 78 stitches.

Round 40: K3, sm, M1R, k7, M1L, sm, k25, work pattern round 2 = 78 stitches.

Round 41: K3, sm, k9, sm, k25, work pattern round 3 = 76 stitches.

Round 42: K3, sm, k9, sm, k25, work pattern round 4 = 74 stitches.

Round 43: K3, sm, M1R, k9, M1L, sm, k25, work pattern round 5 = 74 stitches.

Round 44: K3, sm, k11, sm, k25, work pattern round 6 = 72 stitches.

Round 45: K3, sm, k11, sm, k25, work pattern round 7 = 70 stitches.

Round 46: K3, sm, M1R, k11, M1L, sm, k25, work pattern round 1 = 84 stitches.

Round 47: K3, sm, k13, sm, k25, work pattern round 2 = 82 stitches.

Round 48: K3, sm, k13, sm, k25, work pattern round 3 = 80 stitches.

Round 49: K3, sm, M1R, k13, M1L, sm, k25, work pattern round 4 = 80 stitches.

Round 50: K3, sm, k15, sm, k25, work pattern round 5 = 78 stitches.

Round 51: K3, sm, k15, sm, k25, work pattern round 6 = 76 stitches.

Round 52: K3, sm, M1R, k15, M1L, sm, k25, work pattern round 7 = 76 stitches.

Round 53: K3, sm, k17, sm, k25, work pattern round 1 = 88 stitches.

Round 54: K3, sm, k17, sm, k25, work pattern round 2 = 86 stitches.

Round 55: K3, remove markers and place 17 thumb stitches on scrap yarn. Cast on 9 stitches for the gusset above the thumb opening (green boxes on chart), k25, work pattern round 3 = 76 stitches.

Round 56: K37, work pattern round 4 = 74 stitches.

Round 57: K37, work pattern round 5 = 72 stitches.

Round 58: K37, work pattern round 6 = 70 stitches.

Round 59: K3, ssk, k5, k2tog, k25, work pattern round 7 = 66 stitches.

Round 60: K35, work pattern round 1 = 78 stitches.

Round 61: K35, work pattern round 2 = 76 stitches.

Round 62: K3, ssk, k3, k2tog, k25, work pattern round 3 = 72 stitches.

Round 63: K33, work pattern round 4 = 70 stitches.

Round 64: K33, work pattern round 5 = 68 stitches.

Round 65: K3, ssk, k1, k2tog, k25, work pattern round 6 = 64 stitches.

Round 66: K31, work pattern round 7 = 62 stitches.

Round 67: K31, work pattern round 1 = 74 stitches.

Round 68: K3, sl1, k2tog, psso, k25, work pattern round 2 = 70 stitches.

Round 69: K29, work pattern round 3 = 68 stitches.

Continue working 29 palm stitches plain, and patterned stitches on the back, to round 95.

DECREASING AT THE TOP OF THE RIGHT MITTEN

Round 95: K29, p1, k10, [yo, k1] x 9, yo, k10, p1 = 70 stitches.

Round 96: Ssk, k25, k2tog, p1, k7, k2tog, k21, ssk, k7, p1 = 66 stitches.

Round 97: K27, p1, k6, k2tog, k21, ssk, k6, p1 = 64 stitches.

Round 98: K27, p1, k5, k2tog, k21, ssk, k5, p1 = 62 stitches.

Round 99: K27, p1, k4, k2tog, k21, ssk, k4, p1 = 60 stitches.

Round 100: Ssk, k23, k2tog, p1, k3, k2tog, k21, ssk, k3, p1 = 56 stitches.

Round 101: K25, p1, k2, k2tog, k21, ssk, k2, p1 = 54 stitches.

Round 102: K25, p1, k10, [yo, k1] x 7, yo, k10, p1 = 62 stitches.

Round 103: K25, p1, k7, k2tog, k17, ssk, k7, p1 = 60 stitches.

Round 104: Ssk, k21, k2tog, p1, k6, k2tog, k17, ssk, k6, p1 = 56 stitches.

Round 105: K23, p1, k5, k2tog, k17, ssk, k5, p1 = 54 stitches.

Round 106: K23, p1, k4, k2tog, k17, ssk, k4, p1 = 52 stitches.

Round 107: K23, p1, k3, k2tog, k17, ssk, k3, p1 = 50 stitches.

Round 108: Ssk, k19, k2tog, p1, k2, k2tog, k17, ssk, k2, p1 = 46 stitches.

Round 109: K21, p1, k9, [yo, k1] x 5, yo, k9, p1 = 52 stitches.

Round 110: K21, p1, k6, k2tog, k13, ssk, k6, p1 = 50 stitches.

Round 111: K21, p1, k5, k2tog, k13, ssk, k5, p1 = 48 stitches.

Round 112: Ssk, k17, k2tog, p1, k4, k2tog, k13, ssk, k4, p1 = 44 stitches.

Round 113: K19, p1, k3, k2tog, k13, ssk, k3, p1 = 42 stitches.

Round 114: K19, p1, k2, k2tog, k13, ssk, k2, p1 = 40 stitches.

Round 115: Ssk, k15, k2tog, p1, k1, k2tog, k13, ssk, k1, p1 = 36 stitches.

Round 116: K17, p1, k7, [yo, k1] x 3, yo, k7, p1 = 40 stitches.

Round 117: K17, p1, k4, k2tog, k9, ssk, k4, p1 = 38 stitches.

Round 118: Ssk, k13, k2tog, p1, k3, k2tog, k9, ssk, k3, p1 = 34 stitches.

Round 119: K15, p1, k2, k2tog, k9, ssk, k2, p1 = 32 stitches.

Round 120: Ssk, k11, k2tog, p1, k1, k2tog, k9, ssk, k1, p1 = 28 stitches.

Round 121: Ssk, k9, k2tog, p1, k2tog, k9, ssk, p1 = 24 stitches.

Round 122: Ssk, k7, k2tog, p1, k2tog, k7, ssk, p1 = 20 stitches.

LEFT MITTEN

Round 5: *Yo, k2tog*. Repeat from * to * to end of round.

Rounds 6–10: [P1, k29] x 2.

Rounds 11–17: Work the Peacock's Tail Pattern, k29.

Rounds 18–24: Repeat rounds 11-17.

Round 25: Work pattern round 1, k29 = 72 stitches.

Round 26: Work pattern round 2, k29 = 70 stitches.

Round 27: Work pattern round 3, k29 = 68 stitches.

Round 28: Work pattern round 4, k29 = 66 stitches.

Round 29: Work pattern round 5, k29 = 64 stitches.

Round 30: Work pattern round 6, k29 = 62 stitches.

THUMB GUSSET

Left thumb increases begin on round 31. Place a marker on either side of the increases. The markers are moved between the needles when they are encountered. Always increase on the left side of the first marker and the right side of the second marker.

Round 31: Work pattern round 7, k25, pm, M1R, k1, M1L, pm, k3 = 62 stitches.

Round 32: Work pattern round 1, k25, sm, k3, sm, k3 = 74 stitches.

Round 33: Work pattern round 2, k25, sm, k3, sm, k3 = 72 stitches.

Round 34: Work pattern round 3, k25, sm, M1R, k3, M1L, sm, k3 = 72 stitches.

Round 35: Work pattern round 4, k25, sm, k5, sm, k3 = 70 stitches.

Round 36: Work pattern round 5, k25, sm, k5, sm, k3 = 68 stitches.

Round 37: Work pattern round 6, k25, sm, M1R, k5, M1L, sm, k3 = 68 stitches.

Round 38: Work pattern round 7, k25, sm, k7, sm, k3 = 66 stitches.

Round 39: Work pattern round 1, k25, sm, k7, sm, k3 = 78 stitches.

Round 40: Work pattern round 2, k25, sm, M1R, k7, M1L, sm, k3 = 78 stitches.

Round 41: Work pattern round 3, k25, sm, k9, sm, k3 = 76 stitches.

Round 42: Work pattern round 4, k25, sm, k9, sm, k3 = 74 stitches.

Round 43: Work pattern round 5, k25, sm, M1R, k9, M1L, sm, k3 = 74 stitches.

Round 44: Work pattern round 6, k25, sm, k11, sm, k3 = 72 stitches.

Round 45: Work pattern round 7, k25, sm, k11, sm, k3 = 70 stitches.

Round 46: Work pattern round 1, k25, sm, M1R, k11, M1L, sm, k3 = 84 stitches.

Round 47: Work pattern round 2, k25, sm, k13, sm, k3 = 82 stitches.

Round 48: Work pattern round 3, k25, sm, k13, sm, k3 = 80 stitches.

Round 49: Work pattern round 4, k25, sm, M1R, k13, M1L, sm, k3 = 80 stitches.

Round 50: Work pattern round 5, k25, sm, k15, sm, k3 = 78 stitches.

Round 51: Work pattern round 6, k25, sm, k15, sm, k3 = 76 stitches.

Round 52: Work pattern round 7, k25, sm, M1R, k15, M1L, sm, k3 = 76 stitches.

Round 53: Work pattern round 1, k25, sm, k17, sm, k3 = 88 stitches.

Round 54: Work pattern round 2, k25, sm, k17, sm, k3 = 86 stitches.

Round 55: Work pattern round 3, k25, remove markers and place 17 thumb stitches on scrap yarn. Cast on 9 stitches for the gusset above the thumb opening (green boxes on chart), k3 = 76 stitches.

Round 56: Work pattern round 4, k37 = 74 stitches.

Round 57: Work pattern round 5, k37 = 72 stitches.

Round 58: Work pattern round 6, k37 = 70 stitches.

Round 59: Work pattern round 7, k25, ssk, k5, k2tog, k3 = 66 stitches.

Round 60: Work pattern round 1, k35 = 78 stitches.

Round 61: Work pattern round 2, k35 = 76 stitches.

Round 62: Work pattern round 3, k25, ssk, k3, k2tog, k3 = 72 stitches.

Round 63: Work pattern round 4, k33 = 70 stitches.

Round 64: Work pattern round 5, k33 = 68 stitches.

Round 65: Work pattern round 6, k25, ssk, k1, k2tog, k3 = 64 stitches.

Round 66: Work pattern round 7, k31 = 62 stitches.

Round 67: Work pattern round 1, k31 = 74 stitches.

Round 68: Work pattern round 2, k25, sl1, k2tog, psso, k3 = 70 stitches.

Round 69: Work pattern round 3, k29 = 68 stitches.

Continue working patterned stitches on the back and the 29 palm stitches plain to round 95.

DECREASING AT THE TOP OF THE LEFT MITTEN

Round 95: P1, k10, [yo, k1] x 9, yo, k10, p1, k29 = 70 stitches.

Round 96: P1, k7, k2tog, k21, ssk, k7, p1, ssk, k25, k2tog = 66 stitches.

Round 97: P1, k6, k2tog, k21, ssk, k6, p1, k27 = 64 stitches.

Round 98: P1, k5, k2tog, k21, ssk, k5, p1, k27 = 62 stitches.

Round 99: P1, k4, k2tog, k21, ssk, k4, p1, k27 = 60 stitches.

Round 100: P1, k3, k2tog, k21, ssk, k3, p1, ssk, k23, k2tog = 56 stitches.

Round 101: P1, k2, k2tog, k21, ssk, k2, p1, k25 = 54 stitches.

Round 102: P1, k10, [yo, k1] x 7, yo, k10, p1, k25 = 62 stitches.

Round 103: P1, k7, k2tog, k17, ssk, k7, p1, k25 = 60 stitches.

Round 104: P1, k6, k2tog, k17, ssk, k6, p1, ssk, k21, k2tog = 56 stitches.

Round 105: P1, k5, k2tog, k17, ssk, k5, p1, k23 = 54 stitches.

Round 106: P1, k4, k2tog, k17, ssk, k4, p1, k23 = 52 stitches.

Round 107: P1, k3, k2tog, k17, ssk, k3, p1, k23 = 50 stitches.

Round 108: P1, k2, k2tog, k17, ssk, k2, p1, ssk, k19, k2tog = 46 stitches.

Round 109: P1, k9, [yo, k1] x 5, yo, k9, p1, k21 = 52 stitches.

Round 110: P1, k6, k2tog, k13, ssk, k6, p1, k21 = 50 stitches.

Round 111: P1, k5, k2tog, k13, ssk, k5, p1, k21 = 48 stitches.

Round 112: P1, k4, k2tog, k13, ssk, k4, p1, ssk, k17, k2tog = 44 stitches.

Round 113: P1, k3, k2tog, k13, ssk, k3, p1, k19 = 42 stitches.

Round 114: P1, k2, k2tog, k13, ssk, k2, p1, k19 = 40 stitches.

Round 115: P1, k1, k2tog, k13, ssk, k1, p1, ssk, k15, k2tog = 36 stitches.

Round 116: P1, k7, [yo, k1] x 3, yo, k7, p1, k17 = 40 stitches.

Round 117: P1, k4, k2tog, k9, ssk, k4, p1, k17 = 38 stitches.

Round 118: P1, k3, k2tog, k9, ssk, k3, p1, ssk, k13, k2tog = 34 stitches.

Round 119: P1, k2, k2tog, k9, ssk, k2, p1, k15 = 32 stitches.

Round 120: P1, k1, k2tog, k9, ssk, k1, p1, ssk, k11, k2tog = 28 stitches.

Round 121: P1, k2tog, k9, ssk, p1, ssk, k9, k2tog = 24 stitches.

Round 122: P1, k2tog, k7, ssk, p1, ssk, k7, k2tog = 20 stitches.

FINISHING TOP OF THE MITTEN (BOTH MITTENS)

Close the tops of the mittens by grafting the stitches together or by binding off the stitches on the WS (see the section about finishing, page 31).

THUMB (BOTH MITTENS)

Place the stitches that were held on scrap yarn evenly on two needles. Pick up and knit 9 stitches along the thumb opening = 26 stitches. Knit 22 rounds or 2 in/5 cm.

Round 23: [Ssk, k5, ssk, k4] x 2 = 22 stitches.

Round 24: Knit.

Round 25: [Ssk, k4, ssk, k3] x 2 = 18 stitches.

Round 26: Knit.

Round 27: [Ssk, k3, ssk, k2] x 2 = 14 stitches.

Round 28: [Ssk, k2, ssk, k1] x 2 = 10 stitches.

Round 29: [Ssk, k1, ssk] x 2 = 6 stitches.

Close the top of the thumb in the same way as the top of the mitten.

FINISHING

Weave in all ends. Fold the hem inward and sew it, taking care that the seam is not too tight. Wash and block both mittens, patting them gently to get the right size and to even out the stitches.

Left mitten

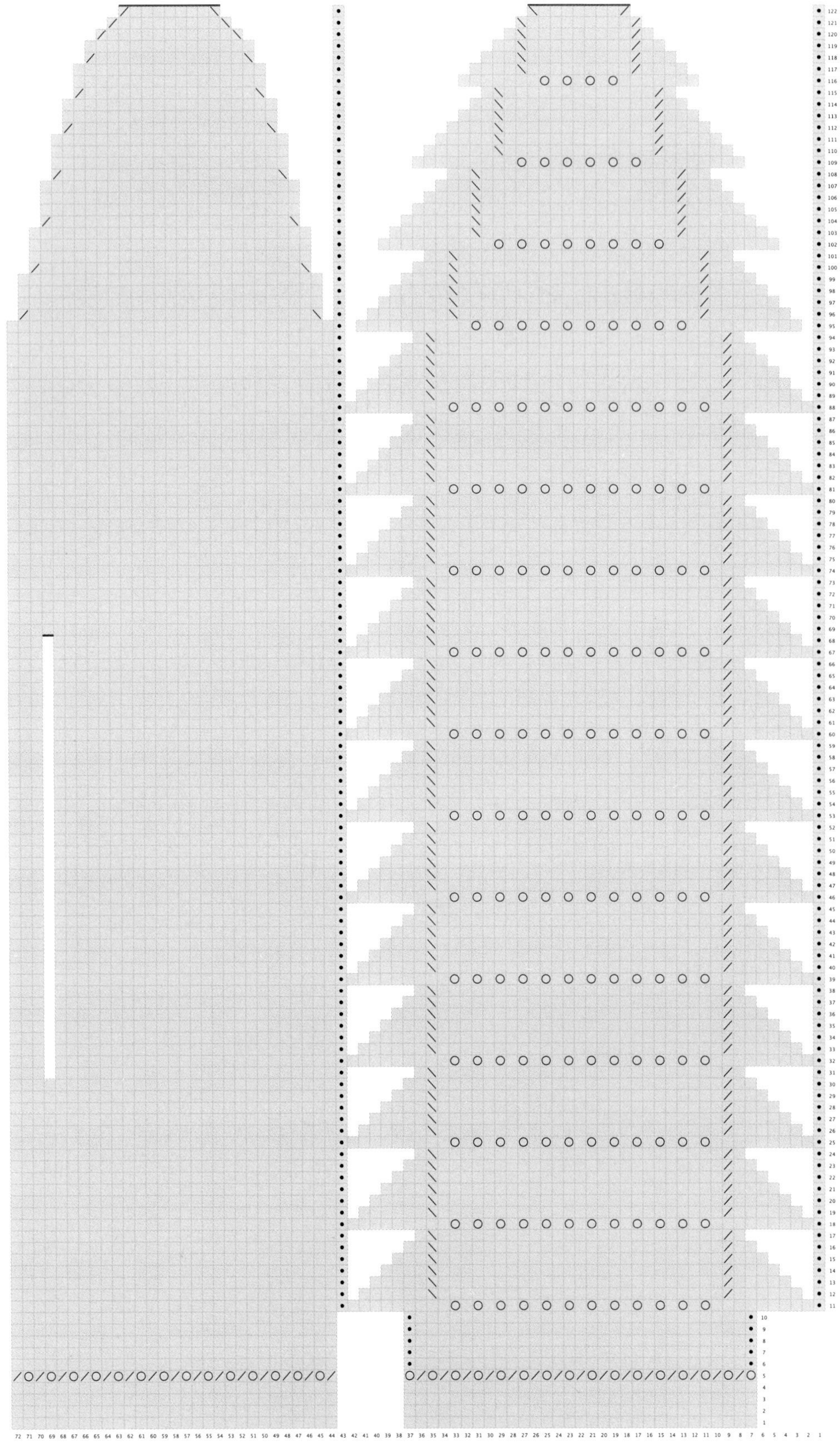

Right mitten

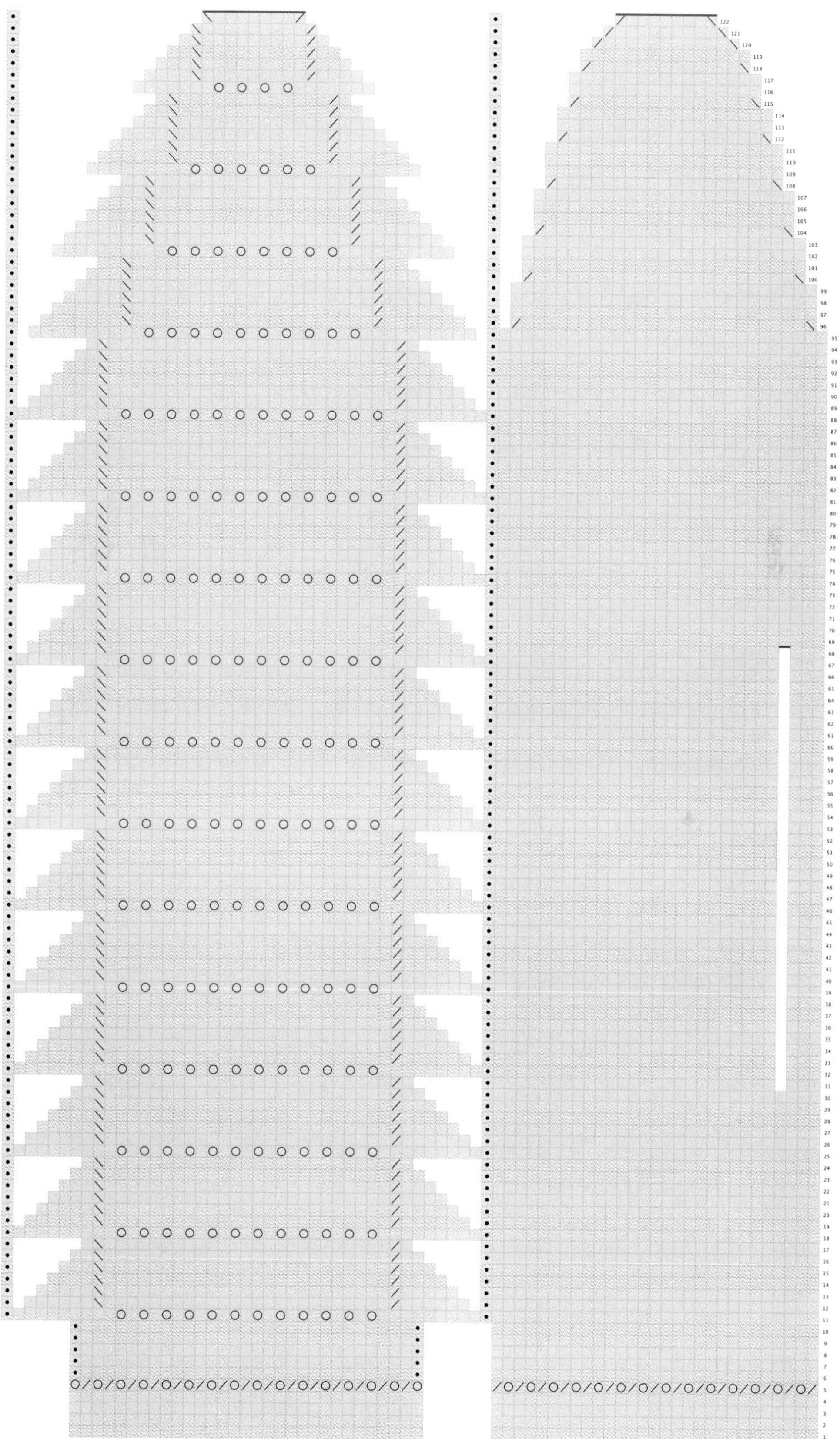

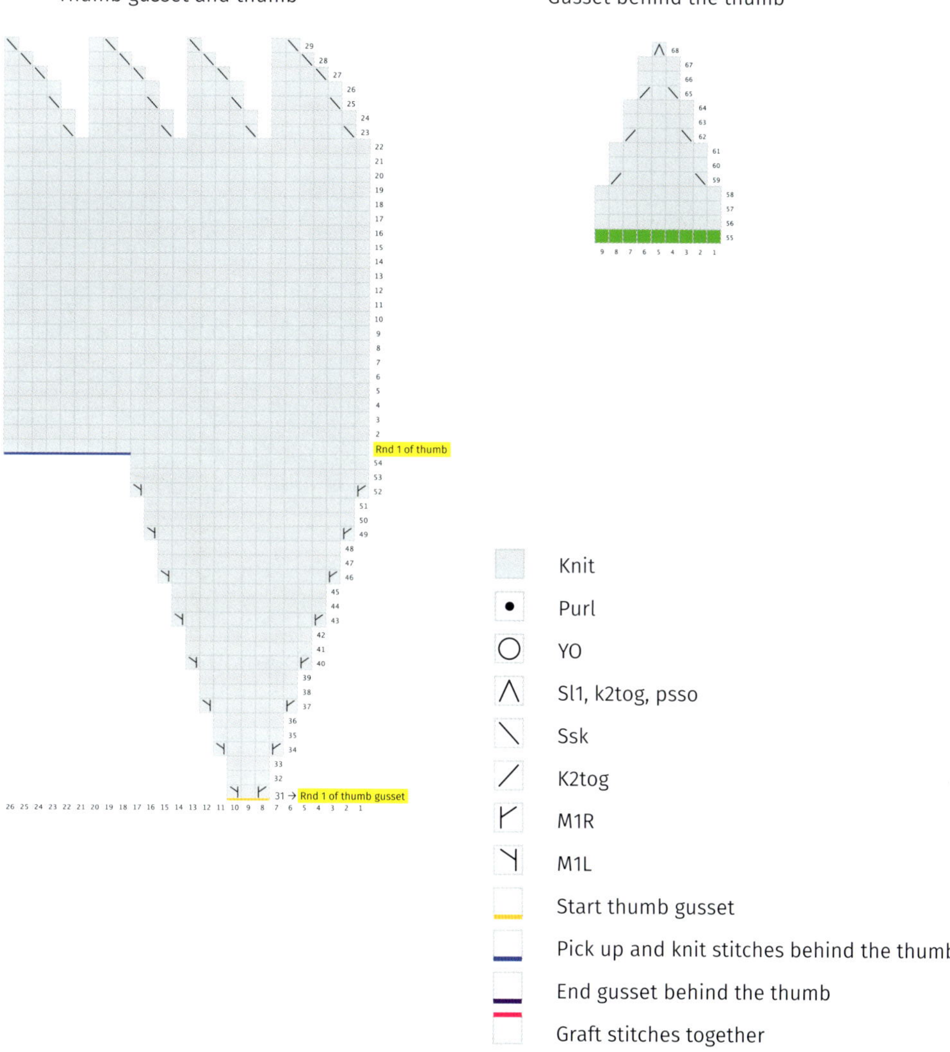
Thumb gusset and thumb
Gusset behind the thumb
Rnd 1 of thumb
31 → Rnd 1 of thumb gusset
Knit
Purl
YO
Sl1, k2tog, psso
Ssk
K2tog
M1R
M1L
Start thumb gusset
Pick up and knit stitches behind the thumb
End gusset behind the thumb
Graft stitches together
CO stitches behind the thumb

YARN INFORMATION

As explained in the discussion of yarn on page 19, the mittens in this book were knitted from three types of yarn: traditional wool yarn (Pirkkalanka, or Finnish Pirkka yarn) in fingering weight (super fine/4-ply), fine tweed yarn, and Mohair 2-ply yarn, which is a blend of goat and merino wools.

Below you'll find a list of yarns that are available in Iceland and are well-suited to knitting the mittens in this book. This is, of course, not an exhaustive list, and some yarns may be difficult to find outside Iceland.

2-ply Jumper Weight from Jamieson & Smith, CYCA #1 (sock/fingering/baby) 100% real Shetland wool, 25g = 115 m/127 yds.

2-ply from Mohair by Canard, CYCA #2 (sport/baby) 65% mohair, 35% merino wool, 50g = 175 m/192 yds.

Admiral 4-ply from Schoppel Wolle, CYCA #1 (sock/fingering/baby) 75% superwash merino wool, 25% nylon, 100g = 420 m/460 yds.

Baby Panda from Rauma, CYCA #1 (sock/fingering/baby) 100% merino wool, 50g = 175 m/192 yds.

Fabel from Drops, CYCA #1 (sock/fingering/baby) 75% wool, 25% polyamide, 50g = 205 m/225 yds.

Fine Tweed from Rowan, CYCA #1 (sock/fingering/baby) 100% wool, 25g = 90 m/99 yds.

Flora from Drops, CYCA #1 (sock/fingering/baby) 65% wool, 35% alpaca, 50g = 210 m/230 yds.

Heritage from Cascade Yarns, CYCA #1 (sock/fingering/baby) 75% superwash merino wool, 25% nylon, 100g = 400 m/438 yds.

Kashwool "socks and more" from Katia, CYCA #1 (sock/fingering/baby) 70% wool, 25% polyamide, 5% cashmere 100g = 410 m/449 yds.

Loft from Brooklyn Tweed, CYCA #1 (sock/fingering/baby) 100% American wool, 50g = 250 m/275 yds.

Merino from Knitting for Olive, CYCA #1 (sock/fingering/baby) 100% organic merino, 50g = 250 m/275 yds.

Merino Yak 4-ply from Regia, CYCA #1 (sock/fingering/baby) 58% wool, 28% polyamide, 14% yak, 100g = 400 m/438 yds.

Milburn 4-ply from Eden Cottage Yarns, CYCA #1 (sock/fingering/baby) 85% British Bluefaced Leicester, 15% silk, 50g = 200 m/220 yds.

Mini Alpakka from Sandnes, CYCA #1 (sock/fingering/baby) 100% alpaca, 50g = 150 m/165 yds.

Mondim from Retrosaria, CYCA #1 (sock/fingering/baby) 100% Portuguese wool, 100g = 385 m/422 yds.

Nord from Drops, CYCA #2 (sport/baby) 45% alpaca, 30% polyamide, 25% wool, 50g = 170 m/186 yds.

Peerie from Brooklyn Tweed, CYCA #1 (sock/fingering/baby) 100% American merino wool, 50g = 192 m/210 yds.

Pip Colorwork from baa ram ewe, CYCA #1 (sock/fingering/baby) 100% British wool, 25g = 116 m/128 yds.

Pirkkalanka Ohut from Pirkka, CYCA #1 (sock/fingering/baby) 100% wool, 100g = 400 m/438 yds.

Valley Tweed from Rowan, CYCA #1 (sock/fingering/baby) 100% wool, 50g = 207 m/227 yds.

Wool Finest from Schoppel Wolle, CYCA #1 (sock/fingering/baby) 100% wool, 100g = 400 m/438 yds.

Yaku 4/16 from CaMaRose, CYCA #1 (sock/fingering/baby) 100% merino wool, 50g = 200 m/220 yds.

Jaipur Silk Fino from BC garn, CYCA #0 (lace/light fingering) 100% silk, 50g = 300 m/328 yds.

Fine Duke Silk from Silkindian, CYCA #1 (sock/fingering/baby) 100% silk, 100g = 366 m/400 yds.

Shetland from Lamana, CYCA #0 (lace/light fingering) 100% wool (superlight), 25g = 140 m/154 yds.

BIBLIOGRAPHY

36 krosssaumsmynztur. (1945). Reykjavík: Garðarshólmi.

Ásdís Jóelsdóttir. (2017). *Íslenska lopapeysan*. Reykjavík: Háskólaútgáfan.

Elsa E. Guðjónsson. (1992). Fágæti úr fylgsnum jarðar. *Skírnir*, Vol. 166, no. 1, 7–40.

Elsa E. Guðjónsson. (2013). Um prjón á Íslandi. *Prjónað úr íslenskri ull*, ed. Oddný S. Jónsdóttir, pp. 9–20. Reykjavík: Vaka-Helgafell.

Elsa. E. Guðjónsson. (1985). Um prjón á Íslandi. *Hugur og hönd*, 8-12. Reykjavík: Heimilisiðnaðarfélag Íslands.

Hélène Magnússon. (2014). *Íslenskt prjón*. Reykjavík: Vaka-Helgafell.

Kristín Harðardóttir. (2012). *Vettlingabókin*. Hafnarfjörður: Tölvusýsl.

Kristín Schmidhauser Jónsdóttir. (1981). *Tvíbandaðir íslenskir vettlingar*. Reykjavík: Heimilisiðnaðarfélag Íslands.

Mynzturbók. (1944). Reykjavík: Íslensk ull.

Vefnaðar og útsaumsgerðir. (1928). Reykjavík: Heimilisiðnaðarfélag Íslands.

Þóra Pjetursdóttir, Jarþrúður Jónsdóttir og Þóra Jónsdóttir. (1886). *Leiðarvísir til að nema ýmsar kvennlegar hannyrðir*. Reykjavík: Printed by Sigurður Guðmundsson.

REFERENCE NUMBER FOR MITTENS IN THE TEXTILE MUSEUM IN BLÖNDUÓS, SEE PHOTOS ON PAGE 5

Ása	HIS-1611
Bára	HB-354
Birta	HIS 139
Björk	HIS-684
Drífa	HB-345
Edda	HB-347
Erla	HIS-725
Freyja	HB-360
Gríma	HB-361
Halla	HIS-2462
Harpa	HB-651
Hildur	HIS-365
Hrefna	HIS-363
Kría	HB-656
Lára	HB-341
Lilja	HIS-1768
Lóa	HB-353
Rúna	HIS-272
Saga	HB-655
Salka	HB-283
Sóley	HIS-2438
Sunna	HB-358
Svala	HB-359
Tinna	HB-650
Vala	HB-652

ACKNOWLEDGMENTS

The models Elín Eva Karlsdóttir and Lamie Panduleni.

The knitters Anna Cynthia Leplar, Guðný Benediktsdóttir, Margrét Sigrún Sigurðardóttir, Rannveig Helgadóttir and Sonja Hilmarsdóttir.

Farmers Market for lending clothes, page 36, 78, 114, 182, 200, 216 and 256.
Geysir for lending clothes, page 48, 86, 129, 149, 156, 166, 174, 187, 208 and 213.

Kría Hjól ehf. for lending a bike for the photography session.

Sólveig Aðalsteinsdóttir for the loan of her dog and her garden for the photography session.

The dogs Tinna and Týra, and a nameless cat who passed by during the photography session.

Videos on www.reykjavikknittingcompany.com:

- Different parts of the mitten
- Making a gauge swatch
- Twisted German cast on
- Knitted cast on
- Stitches, knit, purl, twisted
- Stranded colourwork, dominant and non-dominant colours
- Picking up stitches on side of thumb
- Gusset behind the thumb
- Thumbs, afterthought thumb, thumb with a gusset, side thumb with a gusset
- Increasing
- Decreasing
- Pulling stitches together or pass slip-stitch over method for the top of the mitten
- Grafting stitches together for top of the mitten
- Binding off for top of the mitten
- Finishing and washing

The author and publishers have, insofar as it was possible, attempted to ensure that all patterns are correct and error-free. We sincerely hope that we've been successful in this, but should you encounter any errors, please let us know via email at gudrun.hannele@gmail.com.